Endangere

Linguistic Insights

Studies in Language and Communication

Edited by Maurizio Gotti,
University of Bergamo

Volume 163

ADVISORY BOARD

Vijay Bhatia (Hong Kong)
Christopher Candlin (Sydney)
David Crystal (Bangor)
Konrad Ehlich (Berlin / München)
Jan Engberg (Aarhus)
Norman Fairclough (Lancaster)
John Flowerdew (Hong Kong)
Ken Hyland (Hong Kong)
Roger Lass (Cape Town)
Matti Rissanen (Helsinki)
Françoise Salager-Meyer (Mérida, Venezuela)
Srikant Sarangi (Cardiff)
Susan Šarčević (Rijeka)
Lawrence Solan (New York)
Peter M. Tiersma (Los Angeles)

PETER LANG
Bern · Berlin · Bruxelles · Frankfurt am Main · New York · Oxford · Wien

David Hirsh

Endangered Languages, Knowledge Systems and Belief Systems

PETER LANG
Bern · Berlin · Bruxelles · Frankfurt am Main · New York · Oxford · Wien

Bibliographic information published by die Deutsche Nationalbibliothek
Die Deutsche Nationalbibliothek lists this publication in the Deutsche National-
bibliografie; detailed bibliographic data is available on the Internet
at ‹http://dnb.d-nb.de›.

British Library Cataloguing-in-Publication Data: A catalogue record for this book
is available from The British Library, Great Britain

Library of Congress Cataloging-in-Publication Data

Hirsh, David
 Endangered languages, knowledge systems and belief systems / David Hirsh.
  pages cm – (Linguistic insights : Studies in language and communication,
 ISSN 1424-8689 ; v. 163)
 Includes bibliographical references and index.
 ISBN 978-3-0343-1232-5
 1. Endangered languages. 2. Language and culture. I. Title. II. Series: Linguistic
insights ; v. 163.
 P40.5.E53H57 2013
 408.9–dc23
                    2013035694

ISSN 1424-8689 pb.   ISSN 2235-6371 eBook
ISBN 978-3-0343-1232-5 pb.   ISBN 978-3-0351-0503-2 eBook

© Peter Lang AG, International Academic Publishers, Bern 2013
Hochfeldstrasse 32, CH-3012 Bern, Switzerland
info@peterlang.com, www.peterlang.com, www.peterlang.net

All rights reserved.
All parts of this publication are protected by copyright.
Any utilisation outside the strict limits of the copyright law, without
the permission of the publisher, is forbidden and liable to prosecution.
This applies in particular to reproductions, translations, microfilming,
and storage and processing in electronic retrieval systems.

Printed in Switzerland

Contents

1. Introduction 9
   1.1. Endangered languages 9
   1.2. Language and culture 10
   1.3. Knowledge systems 11
   1.4. Belief systems 13
   1.5. Language policy 14
   1.6. Identity 15
2. Language situation 17
   2.1. Scales of language vitality 20
   2.2. Language situation in Africa 23
      2.2.1. Endangered languages of Nigeria 24
      2.2.2. Endangered languages of Cameroon 25
      2.2.3. Endangered languages of Democratic Republic of the Congo 26
   2.3. Language situation in the Americas 27
      2.3.1. Endangered languages of Mexico 29
      2.3.2. Endangered languages of Brazil 30
      2.3.3. Endangered languages of the United States of America 32
   2.4. Language situation in Asia 35
      2.4.1. Endangered languages of Indonesia 36
      2.4.2. Endangered languages of India 37
      2.4.3. Endangered languages of China 37
   2.5. Language situation in Europe 39
      2.5.1. Endangered languages of the Russian Federation 40
      2.5.2. Endangered languages of Italy 42
      2.5.3. Endangered languages of Germany 42
   2.6. Language situation in the Pacific 43
      2.6.1. Endangered languages of Papua New Guinea 44
      2.6.2. Endangered languages of Australia 45
      2.6.3. Endangered languages of Vanuatu 47

2.7. Summary 48

3. Endangered languages 51
   3.1. Sign languages of North America 52
   3.2. Languages of Alaska 53
   3.3. Languages of South America 54
   3.4. Languages of Thailand 55
   3.5. Languages of Australia 56
   3.6. Languages of Papua New Guinea 57
   3.7. Languages of Vanuatu 59
   3.8. Languages of Russia 60
   3.9. Languages of the Cameroon-Nigeria borderland 60
        3.9.1. The Wawa 61
        3.9.2. The Kwanja 61
        3.9.3. Response to threats 62
   3.10. Languages of Brunei 63
        3.10.1. Iban 63
        3.10.2. Lun Bawang 63
        3.10.3. Response to threats 63
   3.11. Toda language of Southern India 64
   3.12. Summary 66

4. Language policy 67
   4.1. Suppression of indigenous languages 68
        4.1.1. American indigenous languages 68
        4.1.2. Māori 69
   4.2. International and regional declarations 70
        4.2.1. European Charter for Regional or
               Minority Languages 70
        4.2.2. The Universal Declaration of Linguistic Rights ... 70
        4.2.3. UNESCO Universal Declaration on Cultural
               Diversity 71
        4.2.4. First Indigenous Women Summit of the Americas ... 71
        4.2.5. United Nations Declaration of the Rights of
               Indigenous Peoples 72
   4.3. State language policy 72
        4.3.1. India 74

      4.3.2. Indonesia 75
      4.3.3. East Timor 76
      4.3.4. United States 76
      4.3.5. Australia 76
      4.3.6. New Zealand 77
      4.3.7. South Africa 78
      4.3.8. Thailand 79
  4.4. Summary 79
5. Language revitalization 81
  5.1. Saving languages 81
  5.2. Threats to language revitalization 83
  5.3. Bilingualism and multilingualism 84
  5.4. Revival of indigenous languages 87
      5.4.1. Hawaiian 87
      5.4.2. Te Reo Māori 88
      5.4.3. Languages of Thailand 90
      5.4.4. The Iquito dictionary project, Peruvian Amazonia ... 94
      5.4.5. Maintenance of Yi in Yunnan, China 95
      5.4.6. Revitalization of Quechua in Ecuador 96
      5.4.7. Language revitalization in Australia 97
      5.4.8. Welsh 98
      5.4.9. California master-apprentice program 98
  5.5. The future for language revitalization 99
6. Knowledge systems 101
  6.1. Humans and their environment 103
      6.1.1. Forest conservation 103
      6.1.2. Animal conservation 105
  6.2. Health and medicinal knowledge 105
  6.3. Terminology 108
  6.4. Summary 110
7. Belief systems 111
  7.1. Relationship with the land 113
  7.2. Spiritual beliefs 114
  7.3. Traditional health beliefs 116
  7.4. Summary 118

8. Preserving cultural identity 119
   8.1. Cultural identity 119
   8.2. Indigenous education 121
   8.3. Summary 122
9. Conclusion 123
References 129
Index 141
Index of languages 145

1. Introduction

In 2012, I visited an enclave language community in the north of Thailand as part of a research visit to the region. The village had been involved in a language revitalization program for a number of years. I heard from village elders in the community of several hundred individuals of their pride in their heritage language, and of their pride in their cultural traditions. I also heard from the elders of the centrality of their spiritual beliefs to their way of life. For this enclave community, efforts to revitalize their heritage language needed to recognize that their language was not an isolated entity, but rather, it provided a means for the community members to retain their knowledge, beliefs and traditional way of life.

This language community and many other minority language communities in Asia, the Americas, Africa, Europe and the Pacific are struggling to retain their traditional way of life, traditional values and traditional customs in the face of threats presented through contact with more dominant languages and cultures. This book reports on some of these communities to highlight the status of the world's endangered languages, and the knowledge and belief systems held within languages.

1.1. Endangered languages

Michael Krauss, the American linguist credited with highlighting the plight of the world's endangered languages, issued a warning in his address to the Linguistic Society of America held in 1991, that "over half of the world's 6,000 languages will not survive our children's generation. Can we protect our cultural diversity?" (1992a: 10).

Krauss was alarmed at the declining levels of intergenerational transfer of indigenous languages, which signaled to him that many of the world's language were on the path to extinction. For some languages, all the remaining native speakers were over 50 years of age, and the survival of the language was tied to the survival of these remaining speakers. This was the case with Eyak, an Alaskan indigenous language which was facing extinction. In the words of Krauss (1992b: 4):

> The Eyak language of Alaska now has two aged speakers; Mandan has 6, Osage 5, Abenaki-Penobscot 20, and Iowa has 5 fluent speakers. According to counts in 1977, already 13 years ago, Coeur d'Alene had fewer than 20, Tuscarora fewer than 30, Menomini fewer than 50, Yokuts fewer than 10. On and on this sad litany goes, and by no means only for Native North America. Sirenikski Eskimo has two speakers, Ainu is perhaps extinct. Ubykh, the Northwest Caucasian language with the most consonants, 80-some, is nearly extinct, with perhaps only one remaining speaker.

Eyak lost its last native speaker in early 2008. The loss of other languages appears to be inevitable, with no new generations being taught their heritage language. With the loss of each language comes the loss of another language community, and the knowledge and beliefs which once defined its people.

1.2. Language and culture

Since Krauss (1992a) highlighted the plight of many of the world's languages, there has been a rapid growth in research interest in linguistic diversity, language vitality and language revitalization. This recent growth in the body of research builds on a long history of language documentation by field linguists, missionaries and explorers.

The interest in languages is maturing. There is now a body of research linking language knowledge and use with educational opportunities and performance. Links are made between languages and traditional knowledge systems, particularly ecological knowledge associated with forest conservation and the use of medicinal plants. Links are also made between languages and spiritual beliefs.

Languages are increasingly being viewed in terms of the cultures they evolved in, and in terms of the cultural knowledge they carry and the belief systems they are grounded in. Languages are increasingly being viewed as vehicles for the transmission of cultural knowledge from one generation to the next. Attitudes within a language community towards language knowledge and use are increasingly being viewed as indicators of pride in the language, and of community identity.

The link between language and culture is seen in the words of Ken Hale, who wrote the introductory comments to a series of papers on endangered languages which reflected the work of a committed group of linguists at the time: "Language loss in the modern period [...] is part of a much larger process of loss of cultural and intellectual diversity in which politically dominant languages and cultures simply overwhelm indigenous local languages and cultures, placing them in a condition which can only be described as embattled" (1992: 1).

The efforts of minority language communities to retain their identity in the face of pressures to change, both external and internal, are reported in this book. The intention of this book is to allow readers to appreciate languages as vehicles for knowledge systems and belief systems, and as markers for identity. There is a particular focus on indigenous language groups, on the context of language policy change, and on language revitalization efforts.

1.3. Knowledge systems

Knowledge systems are discussed in this book largely in terms of the traditional ecological knowledge of indigenous communities. These knowledge systems reflect accumulated knowledge over time relating to plant species, including use of medicinal plants, animal species, and the natural world. There is a particular focus in this book on sustainable use of the land and its resources.

Berkes provides a definition of traditional ecological knowledge which reflects the interest of this book: "a cumulative body of knowledge and beliefs, handed down through generations by cultural transmission, about the relationship of living beings (including humans) with one another and with their environment" (1993: 3).

As the body of published research on indigenous knowledge systems grows, so too does the body of published work calling for preservation of the knowledge held by indigenous communities about their environment. This knowledge may be of medicinal use of plants, of sustainable use of forest resources, or of the historical significance of geographic locations. There is a realization that language communities need support and encouragement to preserve their knowledge in the face of pressures to modernize and adopt new ways of thinking.

Recognition of the value of this knowledge base by the research community is reflected in the words of Gadgil, Berkes and Folks (1993: 151):

> Where indigenous peoples have depended, for long periods of time, on local environments for the provision of a variety of resources, they have developed a stake in conserving, and in some cases, enhancing, biodiversity. They are aware that biological diversity is a crucial factor in generating the ecological services and natural resources on which they depend.

We are in an era of heightened ecological awareness. We are also in an era of heightened sensitivity to the effect of modernization on indigenous ways of life. The body of knowledge on sustainable use of natural resources is gradually disappearing as indigenous languages move towards extinction. Brosius explains this concept of knowledge as "indigenous understandings of the natural world: systems of classification, how various societies cognize or interpret natural processes, what such groups know about the resources they exploit, and so forth" (1997: 52).

In this context, the loss of knowledge systems can symbolize a loss of a code for human interaction with the natural world, one which seeks to ensure the long-term survival of human, animal and plant species. This code can have a spiritual dimension.

1.4. Belief systems

Belief systems are discussed in this book in terms of spirituality and the relationship between humans, the natural environment and the spiritual world. Bauer (2007: 343) provides this view of belief systems in relation to indigenous communities and cultures:

> Religions worldwide link spirituality with the natural environment. This connection is particularly apparent with regard to the indigenous cultures that have retained much of their heritage. Uncontaminated food and clean water are often directly correlated with survival in these cultures, and the need to preserve this environment is obvious. Clean environments provide sustenance; many indigenous cultures, however, hold the belief that nature also endows their community with distinct relationships involving spiritual beings. Consequently, indigenous beliefs are often dualistic in practice.

There is a link made in Bauer's words between spirituality and the environment. This link can represent people's relationship with the land, and define their customs, values and self-view. It is a link which in colonial times was not so well understood by the colonial powers, but which is now recognized as central to many indigenous belief systems.

Just as languages and knowledge systems are passed from one generation to the next, belief systems also are shared with younger generations through practice and oral traditions. Appiah-Opoku (2007: 82) explains this point:

> Both indigenous knowledge and indigenous beliefs are transmitted through oral tradition, often by storytelling in the context of extended family or a clan system. Both are checked, validated, and revised daily and seasonally through the annual cycle of natural and human activities. Both are often explained through spiritualism, experience, cultural norms, myths, and taboos within a specific geographic context and environment.

The view of belief systems as dynamic assumes that there is scope for indigenous spirituality and customs to adapt as required to ensure continued acceptance by their owners, and to ensure appreciation and acceptance by outsiders.

1.5. Language policy

At the international level, there have been considerable advances in our collective recognition of past failures regarding language policy, and the need to ensure a brighter future for the world's language communities. Some governments have taken the lead in providing high-level recognition of the value of indigenous languages. Some countries have made considerable advances in the educational field, to revitalize languages in decline, in terms of teaching heritage languages in schools and providing instruction in the mother tongue.

Efforts to introduce heritage language instruction into schools to cater for indigenous children ideally need to take account of the values and beliefs of the children so as to ensure community support. At the same time, there may be community pressure to provide the indigenous students with the same educational opportunities as mainstream students. There is an important role for indigenous teachers in this context, to provide educational opportunities for indigenous students through a familiar language and a familiar paradigm of learning. Bilingual, multilingual and mother tongue-based educational programs are going through challenging, and exciting, times.

1.6. Identity

The stories told in this book are of some communities successfully passing their language, knowledge and beliefs onto future generations. Stories are also told of languages, knowledge systems and belief systems which are not being successfully maintained and transmitted.

There are multiple threats to language and culture. There is the threat of language shift towards more dominant languages, particularly those with higher political or social status in the region or country, or those which are viewed as necessary or beneficial for economic or social development. There is the threat to traditional ecological knowledge from regional and state policy and practice concerning land use and conservation. This is often described in terms of traditional versus modern approaches to agriculture, forest use and conservation. There is the threat to belief systems presented by more dominant communities and the belief systems and religious practices they promote.

For each remaining endangered language, there is a chance of revitalization of the language, knowledge system and belief system, as long as native speakers, and their potential to provide guidance and leadership, remain. One key factor in the success of language revitalization programs appears to be the attitude of the community towards their language, and how this reflects their identity. In identifying strongly with their heritage language, language users are providing a strong foundation upon which language revival can take place, to reverse patterns of language loss.

2. Language situation

There is an abundance of languages in the world, resulting from migration (forced and voluntary), settlement, social contact and social isolation. New languages continue to be reported in the literature, but it may be too late to save some of these newly documented languages from extinction.

The Ethnologue (Lewis *et al.* 2013) comprehensively lists all known living languages in the world. The work, which reflects the meticulous activities of field linguists, ethnographers and cartographers, among other experts, identifies 7,105 living languages. Asia is home to the largest number of living languages (2,304), followed by Africa (2,146), the Pacific (1,311), the Americas (1,060) and Europe (284). Graph 1 represents this geographic distribution of the world's languages.

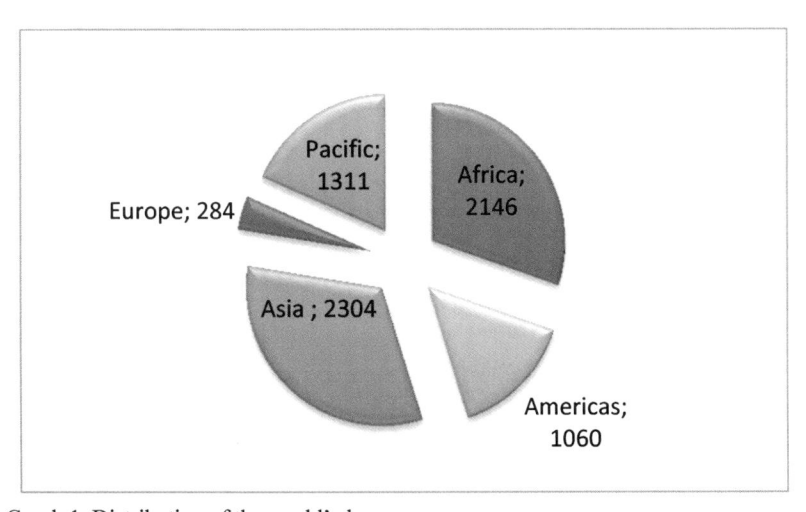

Graph 1. Distribution of the world's languages.

Languages are not evenly distributed across the globe, with some regions being more linguistically diverse than others. Papua New Guinea is the most linguistically diverse country, with 836 documented living languages. Vanuatu, Solomon Islands and the Central African Republic are other examples of linguistically diverse countries. At the other extreme, Samoa, Cuba, Haiti, San Marino, British Indian Ocean Territory and North Korea are among the world's least linguistically diverse countries/territories (Lewis *et al.* 2013: 39-45).

There are regions of the world with large concentrations of languages. This is evident in the following list of countries, each with over 100 documented living languages (sourced from Lewis *et al.* 2013).

Country	Number of living languages
Papua New Guinea	836
Indonesia	706
Nigeria	522
India	447
China	298
Mexico	282
Cameroon	280
Brazil	215
Australia	214
United States of America	214
Democratic Republic of Congo	212
Philippines	181
Malaysia	138
Chad	130
Tanzania	121
Vanuatu	116
Viet Nam	111
Nepal	110
Myanmar	109
Russian Federation	103

Table 1. Countries with over 100 documented languages.

This list includes countries with relatively small populations. Papua New Guinea has 836 documented languages spread across a population of seven million, while Vanuatu has 116 languages and a population of 245,600. These two countries are the most linguistically diverse. The list also includes countries with comparatively large populations, including Indonesia which has 706 documented languages spread across a population of 242 million, Nigeria with 522 languages and a population of 162 million, India with 447 languages and a population of 1.241 billion, and China with 298 languages and a population of 1.344 billion. The list includes countries such as Australia (population 22 million) and the United States of America (population 311 million) where most of the indigenous languages are endangered or near extinction.

Of the 7,105 documented languages in the world, nine languages have over 100 million speakers (Chinese, Spanish, Hindi, English, Arabic, Portuguese, Bengali, Russian and Japanese), and a further 385 languages have over one million speakers. There are an additional 4,710 languages with between 1,000 and 999,999 speakers, 1,054 languages with between 100 and 999 speakers, 340 languages with between ten and 99 speakers, and 134 languages with between one and nine remaining speakers (Lewis *et al.* 2013).

Nettle and Romaine (2000) reflect on the vast linguistic diversity in Papua New Guinea where, they estimate, up to 80% of the known languages have fewer than 5,000 speakers, and possibly a third of the known languages have fewer than 500 speakers. This is assumed to be a stable feature of language distribution in Papua New Guinea, and can be explained not in terms of isolation but in terms of social contact between groups. The theory presented in Nettle and Romaine (2000) is that self-sufficiency allowed small settlements to flourish, while social contact between groups gave rise to heightened awareness of the desirability of distinctiveness of languages to enhance the social capital associated with membership of a language community. In other words, there appears to have been a human intent to create and maintain distinctions between languages, while multilingualism allowed for communication between groups.

2.1. Scales of language vitality

Language vitality is viewed in degrees. Fishman (1991) devised an eight-level Graded Intergenerational Disruption Scale for languages, which is represented as follows, where level one is the safest and level eight is the most threatened:

1. The language is used in education, work, mass media and government at the nationwide level.
2. The language is used for local and regional mass media and governmental services.
3. The language is used for local and regional work by both insiders and outsiders.
4. Literacy in the language is transmitted through education.
5. The language is used orally by all generations and is effectively used in written form throughout the community.
6. The language is used orally by all generations and is being learned by children as their first language.
7. The child-bearing generation knows the language well enough to use it with their elders but is not transmitting it to their children.
8. The only remaining speakers of the language are members of the grandparent generation.

Similar graded categories have been adopted by UNESCO in their Language Vitality and Endangerment Framework (see Moseley 2010), as follows:

1. Safe: the language is spoken by all generations; intergenerational transmission is uninterrupted.
2. Vulnerable: most children speak the language, but it may be restricted to certain domains (e.g., the home).
3. Definitely endangered: children no longer learn the language as the mother tongue in the home.

4. Severely endangered: the language is spoken by grandparents; while the parent generation may understand it, they do not speak it to children or among themselves.
5. Critically endangered: the youngest speakers are grandparents and older, and they speak the language partially and infrequently.
6. Extinct: there are no speakers left.

The Expanded Graded Intergenerational Disruption Scale (Lewis and Simons 2010) is used for reporting language status in the Ethnologue (Lewis *et al.* 2013). This scale identifies the following levels:

0. International: The language is widely used between nations in trade, knowledge exchange, and international policy.
1. National: The language is used in education, work, mass media, and government at the national level.
2. Provincial: The language is used in education, work, mass media, and government within major administrative subdivisions of a nation.
3. Wider Communication: The language is used in work and the mass media without official status to transcend language differences across a region.
4. Educational: The language is in vigorous use, with standardization and literature being sustained through a widespread system of institutionally supported education.
5. Developing: The language is in vigorous use, with literature in a standardized form being used by some, though this is not yet widespread or sustainable.
6. (a) Vigorous: The language is used for face-to-face communication by all generations and the situation is sustainable.
   (b) Threatened: The language is used for face-to-face communication within all generations, but it is losing users.
7. Shifting: The child-bearing generation can use the language among themselves, but it is not being transmitted to children.
8. (a) Moribund: The only remaining active users of the language are members of the grandparent generation and older.

(b) Nearly Extinct: The only remaining users of the language are members of the grandparent generation or older who have little opportunity to use the language.
9. Dormant: The language serves as a reminder of heritage identity for an ethnic community, but no one has more than symbolic proficiency.
10. Extinct: The language is no longer used and no one retains a sense of ethnic identity associated with the language.

Language vitality, as suggested in these scales, is shaped by a range of factors, particularly: (1) language and culture policy, and the status and rights attached to the language and culture at the local and national level; (2) rights attached to traditional land ownership and use; (3) the attitudes of speakers towards their heritage language and culture; and (4) the domains where the language is used, with importance attached to use of the language in the home and the local school.

The number of speakers is not always a reliable indicator of language vitality. While languages are being successfully passed on to future generations, even small communities may enjoy strong language vitality over time. This is the case for many Papuan language communities which exist in close contact with neighboring language communities.

The age of the youngest speakers is a strong indicator of language vitality. For some of the Alaskan languages reported by Krauss where intergenerational transmission of the language had been abandoned, the life expectancy of the language was tied to the life expectancy of its remaining speakers. This disruption in language use is associated with a shift to a more dominant language, the reasons for which will be reported in subsequent chapters of this book.

The following is a view of the language situation in Africa, the Americas, Asia, Europe and the Pacific. Data sourced from the online Ethnologue (Lewis *et al.* 2013) have in turn been sourced from SIL International (formerly the Summer Institute of Linguistics) linguists, studies carried out by field linguists and ethnographers, compilers and contributors to languages atlases of regions of the world, and census results carried out within state territories.

2.2. Language situation in Africa

Africa is home to 2,146 living languages, of which 1,800 are safe and 346 are endangered (Lewis *et al.* 2013), and a further 46 languages of Africa are listed as extinct (Whalen/Simons 2012) (see Graph 2).

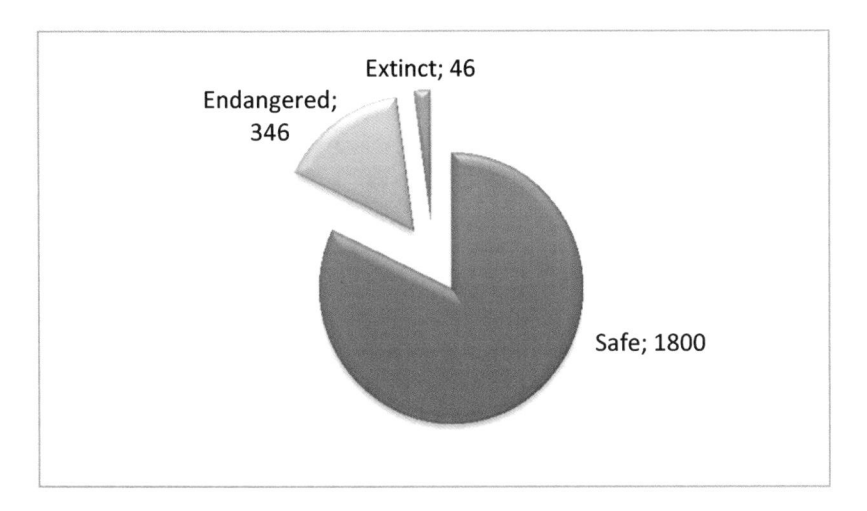

Graph 2. Language situation in Africa.

Crystal (2010) reports that the four main language families of Africa are:

- Niger-Congo (1350 languages)
- Nilo-Saharan (180 languages)
- Khoisan (40 languages)
- Afro-Asiatic (300 languages)

Over 95% of the languages of Africa have fewer than one million speakers. In this linguistic landscape, regional lingua francas have evolved in Africa to provide a means of communication between different language groups. These lingua francas, and their domains, include:

- Arabic (used in North and Northeast Africa)
- Kiswahili (used in East Africa)
- English (used in former British colonies)
- French (used in former French colonies)
- Hausa (used in West and Central Africa)
- Bombara-Malinka (used in West and Central Africa)
- Wolof (used in West and Central Africa)
- Kikongo (used in West and Central Africa)
- Lingala (used in West and Central Africa)
- Pidgin English (used in West and Central Africa)
- Krio (used in West and Central Africa)
- Songo (in West and Central Africa)

Lodhi (1993) reports that Arabic is the most widely used language on the African continent with 110 million speakers, followed by Hausa-Fulani, Oromo/Galla and Kiswahili, each with 20-30 million speakers. The languages of Africa with small numbers of speakers compete with the local, national and colonial languages.

Errington (2008: 85) recounts that, in former times in the Senegambia region of Africa's eastern coast, neighboring communities spoke three different languages, Fula, Wolof and Sereer, which distinguished the communities along cultural and religious lines. In this respect, language diversity can be partly explained by the presence of multiple cultural groups, and the use of language to identify membership of these different groups.

Within Africa, the countries with the highest number of documented living languages are Nigeria, Cameroon, and the Democratic Republic of the Congo. There three countries will be looked at in turn.

2.2.1. Endangered languages of Nigeria

Nigeria has 522 living languages, of which an estimated 59 are endangered. While English, the former colonial language, is the official language of Nigeria, a multitude of regional languages are widely used, particularly outside the large urban centers. These include Afro-Asiatic languages including Hausa, and Niger-Congo languages including Yoruba and Igbo. These three regional languages have been constitutionally recognized as major languages (Adegbija 2004).

The endangered languages of Nigeria include the following 15 most critically endangered languages, with the most recent estimate of remaining number of native speakers provided (sourced from Lewis *et al.* 2013):

- Akum (unknown; nearly extinct)
- Baissa Fali (few remaining speakers)
- Barikanchi (no known native speakers)
- Bassa-Kontagora (10)
- Damakawa' (no known native speakers)
- Gamo-Ningi (no known native speakers)
- Kubi (no known native speakers)
- Lere (unknown; nearly extinct)
- Njerep (6)
- Sambe (6)
- Shau (unknown; nearly extinct)
- Sheni (6)
- Usaghade (unknown)
- Zari (no known native speakers)
- Ziriya (no known native speakers)

2.2.2. Endangered languages of Cameroon

Cameroon has 280 living languages, of which an estimated 66 are endangered. The official languages of Cameroon are French and English, reflecting the influence of former European colonial powers in Africa. Major lingua francas in Cameroon are Pidgin English, Fulfulde and Beti, while minor lingua francas are Arab Shuwa, Basaa, Bulu, Duala, Hausa, Kanuri, Mungaka and Wandala, each operating within a defined geographic location (Kouega 2007).

The endangered languages of Cameroon include the following twelve most critically endangered languages, with the most recent estimate of remaining number of native speakers provided (sourced from Lewis *et al.* 2013):

- Baldemu (4)
- Bung (3)
- Busuu (8)
- Gey (no known native speakers)
- La'bi (no known native speakers)
- Leti (no known native speakers)
- Luo (1)
- Ndai (5)
- Nimbari (no known native speakers)
- Oblo (unknown; nearly extinct)
- To (no known native speakers in Cameroon)
- Zhoa (unknown)

2.2.3. Endangered languages of Democratic Republic of the Congo

The Democratic Republic of the Congo has 212 living languages, of which an estimated 13 are endangered. The official language taken from colonial times is French, while four indigenous languages have provincial language status and are regarded as national languages. These are Ciluba, Kikongo, Kiswahili and Lingala. They provide for inter-group communication in their areas of influence and operate as regional lingua francas. In addition, English is establishing itself in a more prominent role (Kasanga 2010).

The endangered languages of Democratic Republic of the Congo include the following two most critically endangered languages, with the most recent estimate of remaining number of native speakers provided (sourced from Lewis *et al.* 2013):

- Boguru (unknown; nearly extinct)
- Hungana (400)

Africa is a complex linguistic landscape. In addition to the local and regional languages are languages which are afforded official status.

Lodhi (1993) describes Africa as a linguistic map with these parts: Anglophone, Francophone, Lusophone, Arabiphone and Swahiliphone. Combinations of colonial and African languages are widely used for administration and afforded official status. Clearly, bilingual and multilingual education programs are required in Africa to enable local languages to operate and survive alongside the more dominant languages.

2.3. Language situation in the Americas

The Americas are home to 1060 living languages, of which 417 are safe and 643 are endangered (Lewis *et al.* 2013). A further 183 are listed as extinct (Whalen/Simons 2012) (see Graph 3).

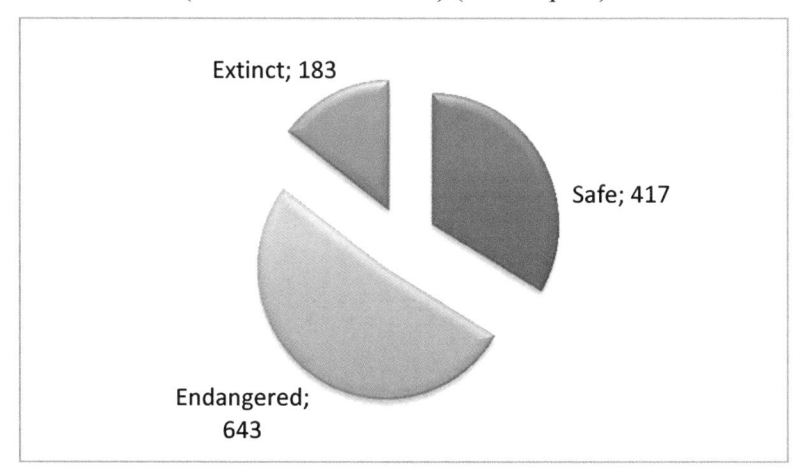

Graph 3. Language situation in the Americas.

Crystal (2010) indicates that 300 languages were once spoken by indigenous people in North America. Today, only 50 have more than 1,000 speakers, and only a small number have more than 10,000 speakers. These 300 indigenous languages of North America have been classified into 50 families:

- Eskimo-Aleut: Yup'ik (Alaskan, Siberian) and Inupiaq (Inuit or Inuktitut)
- Na-Dene (50 languages spoken in Alaska, northwest Canada, and south-west-central US)
- Alonquian (30 languages)
- Mayan (30 languages spoken in Mexico and Central America)
- Itokan (20 languages spoken in western and south-west US and Mexico)
- Uto-Aztecan (few speakers today)
- Tanoan languages

There are 250 indigenous languages of Meso-American spoken in Central America. The main languages of Meso-America are:

- Zapotec (450,000 speakers)
- Otomi (250,000 speakers)
- Mixtec (250,000 speakers)

In addition, there are indigenous languages of Central and South America which can be grouped as:

- Chibchan: 20 languages spoken in Central America, Columbia, Venezuela, Bolivia and Brazil
- Ge-Pano-Carib: 200 languages spoken in the Andes and along the Brazilian Amazon Basin
- Andean-Equatorial: 250 languages spoken in Central America, Southern Brazil and the Andes

Reyes (2009) reports that the minority language groups in the Americas face complex sociolinguistic situations, in which external expectations of immersion into the dominant culture are often high. These expectations can negatively impact on heritage language use and identity. Nevertheless, in countries or regions where English, French, Spanish or Portuguese are the medium of instruction and learning in most schools, local languages may be in use in local schools if teachers are drawn from the local community. The background, language knowledge and identity of school teachers are thus important dimensions in the efforts to maintain local language use.

England (2007) reports that 21 Mayan languages are spoken in Guatemala. The official language in Guatemala is Spanish. There has been language shift from local languages to Spanish to the extent that many children now do not speak their heritage language. There has been a focus on increasing the domains in which the Mayan languages are spoken in Guatemala, covering writing, including school texts, bilingual education programs and the training of a body of Mayan-speaking linguists.

In the Americas, the countries with the highest number of documented living languages are Mexico, Brazil and the United States of America. These three countries will be looked at in turn.

2.3.1. Endangered languages of Mexico

Mexico has 282 living languages, of which an estimated 113 are endangered. Spanish is the de facto official language and the mother tongue of 90% of the population. At the time of independence in 1810, around 30% of the population spoke Spanish. By 1895, only 17% of the population spoke indigenous languages. Indigenous languages have recently been afforded status as national languages alongside Spanish in an effort to recognize the importance these languages held in pre-colonial times (Terborg/Landa/Moore 2006).

The endangered languages of Mexico include the following nine most critically endangered languages, with the most recent estimate of remaining number of native speakers provided (sourced from Lewis *et al.* 2013):

- Chiapanec (no known native speakers)
- Chicomuceltec (no known native speakers)
- Chinantec, Chiltepec (a few older speakers)
- Cochimi (no known native speakers)

- Ixcatec (21)
- Kiliwa (10)
- Mixtec, Sindihui (34)
- Tarahumara, Northern (1)
- Zoque, Tabasco (40)

2.3.2. Endangered languages of Brazil

Brazil has 215 living languages, of which an estimated 152 are endangered. Brazil, the only Portuguese-speaking country in the Americas, has, at least domestically, tended to overlook its linguistic diversity until recently, viewing itself as a Portuguese speaking nation. Since colonial times, Brazil followed a policy of repression of indigenous languages in schools, to ensure the learning of Portuguese (Massini-Cagliari 2003).

The endangered languages of Brazil include the following 49 most critically endangered languages, with the most recent estimate of remaining number of native speakers provided:

- Amanayé (no known native speakers)
- Apiaká (1)
- Arapaso (no known native speakers)
- Arára, Mato Grosso (no known native speakers)
- Atorada (few native speakers in Brazil)
- Baré (spoken by a few elders)
- Chiquitano (unknown)
- Cocama-Cocamilla (unknown; nearly extinct)
- Gavião, Pará (unknown)
- Guana (no known native speakers)
- Jabutí (1)
- Kaimbé (no known native speakers)
- Kamba (no known native speakers)
- Kambiwá (no known native speakers)
- Kapinawá (no known native speakers)
- Karirí-Xocó (no known native speakers)
- Katukína (no known native speakers)

- Kaxuiâna (no known native speakers)
- Lakondê (1)
- Matipuhy (no known native speakers)
- Miranha (no known native speakers)
- Miriti (no known native speakers)
- Nukuini (no known native speakers)
- Omagua (no known native speakers)
- Pankararú (no known native speakers)
- Paranawát (no known native speakers)
- Patamona (unknown)
- Pataxó Hã-Ha-Hãe (no known native speakers)
- Potiguára (no known native speakers)
- Poyanáwa (no known native speakers)
- Tapeba (no known native speakers)
- Tawandê (unknown)
- Tingui-Boto (no known native speakers)
- Torá (no known native speakers)
- Tremembé (no known native speakers)
- Truká (no known native speakers)
- Tupinikin (no known native speakers)
- Turiwára (no known native speakers)
- Tuxá (no known native speakers)
- Uamué (no known native speakers)
- Umotína (1)
- Wakoná (no known native speakers)
- Wasu (no known native speakers)
- Xakriabá (no known native speakers)
- Xetá (no known native speakers)
- Xipaya (1)
- Xiriâna (no known native speakers)
- Xukurú (no known native speakers)
- Yabaâna (no known native speakers)

2.3.3. Endangered languages of the United States of America

The United States of America (US) has 214 living languages of which an estimated 199 are endangered. The US is linguistically shaped by high rates of immigration, bringing in over 200 new languages. These immigrant languages are not included in the count of 214 languages. English dominates the linguistic landscape of the US despite the rising number of non-English speakers and the rising call for bilingual and multilingual modes of education to accommodate and preserve the linguistic diversity (Shell 1993).

There has been a widespread shift away from indigenous language use in the US towards English in recent times. Crawford (2000) reports, as an example, on the Navajo of Rough Rock and Rock Point in Arizona. In the 1970s, over 95% of children spoke Navajo as their first language with little knowledge of English. Recently, the estimate was 50% of Navajo children speaking Navajo as their first language. The shift away from Navajo towards English was reflected in the low status associated with Navajo among Navajo teenagers.

The endangered languages of the US include the following 67 most critically endangered languages, with the most recent estimate of remaining number of native speakers provided (sourced from Lewis *et al.* 2013):

- Abenaki, Eastern (no known native speakers)
- Abenaki, Western (no known native speakers)
- Afro-Seminole Creole (unknown)
- Apache, Lipan (no known native speakers)
- Atsugewi (no known native speakers)
- Barbareño (unknown)
- Catawba (unknown)
- Chehalis, Lower (no known native speakers)
- Chehalis, Upper (no known native speakers)
- Chitimacha (no known native speakers)
- Coos (no known native speakers)
- Cruzeño (no known native speakers)
- Cupeño (no known native speakers)

- Esselen (no known native speakers)
- Eyak (no known native speakers)
- Hawai'i Pidgin Sign Language (a few users)
- Ineseño (no known native speakers)
- Iowa-Oto (no known native speakers)
- Kansa (no known native speakers)
- Kato (no known native speakers)
- Kitsai (no known native speakers)
- Klamath-Modoc (no known native speakers)
- Lumbee (no known native speakers)
- Maidu, Northeast (1)
- Mattole (no known native speakers)
- Miami (no known native speakers)
- Miwok, Coast (no known native speakers)
- Miwok, Lake (1)
- Miwok, Northern Sierra (no known native speakers)
- Miwok, Plains (no known native speakers)
- Mohegan-Pequot (no known native speakers)
- Nanticoke (no known native speakers)
- Narragansett (no known native speakers)
- Nisenan (no known native speakers)
- Nomlaki (unknown)
- Nooksack (no known native speakers)
- Nottoway (no known native speakers)
- Obispeño (no known native speakers)
- Ohlone, Northern (unknown)
- Ohlone, Southern (no known native speakers)
- Patwin (unknown)
- Plains Indian Sign Language (unknown)
- Pomo, Eastern (unknown)
- Pomo, Northeastern (no known native speakers)
- Pomo, Northern (1)
- Pomo, Southern (unknown)
- Powhatan (no known native speakers)
- Purisimeño (no known native speakers)
- Quileute (no known native speakers)
- Quinault (no known native speakers)

- Salinan (no known native speakers)
- Salish, Straits (5 in the United States)
- Serrano (no known native speakers)
- Shasta (no known native speakers)
- Siuslaw (no known native speakers)
- Tolowa (1)
- Tonkawa (no known native speakers)
- Tunica (no known native speakers)
- Twana (no known native speakers)
- Unami (no known native speakers)
- Ventureño (no known native speakers)
- Wampanoag (no known native speakers)
- Wichita (1)
- Wintu (no known native speakers)
- Wiyot (no known native speakers)
- Wyandot (no known native speakers)
- Yuki (no known native speakers)

Reyes (2009) reflects on the scope for bilingualism in the Americas, indicating that the debate in Mexico, for example, has centered around the questions of whether members of indigenous communities should be forced to assimilate and give up their ethnic identity and language in order to become accepted citizens of the nation, and whether indigenous peoples could integrate into and acquire full membership in the dominant society while simultaneously preserving and fostering their own identity and diversity. Similar questions are raised elsewhere in the Americas, often in response to language revitalization efforts and programs. The response to these questions has an influence on the success of language revitalization programs, the extent of heritage language learning and use in schools, and the status afforded to minority languages in the wider community.

2.4. Language situation in Asia

Asia is home to 2,304 living languages, of which 1,441 are safe and 863 are endangered (Lewis *et al.* 2013), and a further 47 are listed as extinct (Whalen/Simons 2012) (see Graph 4).

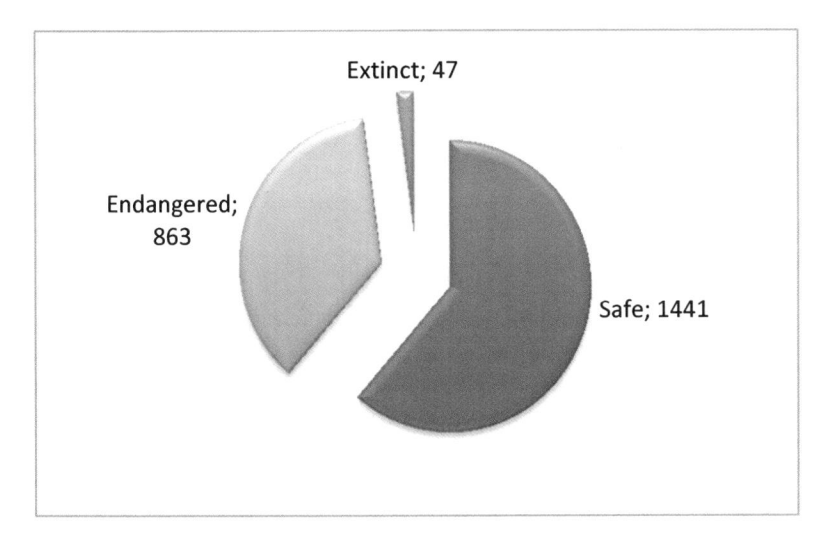

Graph 4. Language situation in Asia.

Joseph (2004) highlights the link between language and national identity, and the development of national language identity in modern Asia. The former role of English, French, and other European languages in the administration of parts of Asia has been replaced in many contexts by national languages of Asia, as an expression of national identity. The use of national languages in this role has, in many countries, had a negative impact on the status of minority languages in education and society in general, pushing many languages towards extinction.

Within Asia, the countries with the highest number of documented living languages are Indonesia, India and China. These countries will be looked at in turn.

2.4.1. Endangered languages of Indonesia

Indonesia has 706 living languages, of which an estimated 301 are endangered. Paauw (2009) explains that Indonesia, a former Dutch colony, has been promoting an indigenous language policy, selecting Bahasa Indonesia as its national language and recognizing the importance of indigenous vernaculars.

The endangered languages of Indonesia include the following 25 most critically endangered languages, with the most recent estimate of remaining number of native speakers provided (sourced from Lewis *et al.* 2013):

- Bengkala Sign Language (41)
- Chinese, Min Dong (unknown)
- Duriankere (30)
- Dusner (no known native speakers)
- Ibu (35)
- Iha-based Pidgin (no known native speakers)
- Javindo (no known native speakers)
- Kamarian (no known native speakers)
- Kanum, Bädi (10)
- Kayeli (no known native speakers)
- Kembra (20)
- Kwerisa (15)
- Lengilu (3)
- Liki (11)
- Malay, Bacanese (6)
- Mander (20)
- Masimasi (10)
- Massep (25)
- Mor (30)
- Namla (30)
- Nusa Laut (no known native speakers)
- Onin Based Pidgin (no known native speakers)
- Petjo (unknown; nearly extinct)
- Tandia (no known native speakers)
- Woria (5)

2.4.2. Endangered languages of India

India has 447 living languages, of which an estimated 48 are endangered. The languages of India belong to four linguistic families: Indo-Aryan, Dravidian, Austro-Asiatic and Tibeto-Chinese. In this complex linguistic landscape mirroring a complex cultural and religious landscape, there has been an effort, since independence, to promote Hindi as a unifying language, with limited success. In addition to Hindi, English plays a central role in education, while regional languages have received official status due to their importance regionally (Oommen 2003).

The endangered languages of India include the following 15 most critically endangered languages, with the most recent estimate of remaining number of native speakers provided (sourced from Lewis *et al.* 2013):

- Ahom (no known native speakers)
- Chamling (unknown)
- Great Andamanese, Mixed (7)
- Khamyang (50)
- Koraga, Mudu (unknown)
- Kulung (unknown)
- Malaryan (no known native speakers)
- Manna-Dora (unknown)
- Nefamese (unknown)
- Pali (no known native speakers)
- Parenga (unknown; nearly extinct)
- Rangkas (no known native speakers)
- Ruga (unknown; nearly extinct)
- Ullatan (no known native speakers)
- Urali (no known native speakers)

2.4.3. Endangered languages of China

China has 298 living languages, of which an estimated 108 are endangered. There are 56 recognized nationalities in China, including the Han Chinese and 55 national minorities, and these are recognized in language policy in China. Aside from the central unifying role attributed to Standard Chinese, or *Pǔtōnghuà*, there is provision for teaching and use of the selected minority languages, including Hui (Chinese Moslem), Man (Manchu), Menggu (Mongol), Miao, Uighur, Yi, Zang (Tibetan) and Zhuang (Bradley 2005). Bradley (2006) reports that the identification of 55 national minorities in China overlooks the vast linguistic diversity present in China.

The endangered languages of China include the following nine most critically endangered languages, with the most recent estimate of remaining number of native speakers provided (sourced from Lewis *et al.* 2013):

- A'ou (50)
- Ayizi (50)
- Gelao, Re (a few speakers)
- Khakas (10 in China)
- Lawu (50)
- Manchu (20)
- Mulao (a few elderly speakers)
- Nanai (40 in China)
- Qabiao (18 in China)

Joseph (2004) highlights how national, ethnic and religious identities have been constructed through language. The role of language in defining the identities of peoples within a country has shaped language policy and use across Asia. Some countries have adopted a secular, multilingual approach to language policy. Other countries in Asia have seen a national or state language used to define the identity of its people, to the detriment of minority languages. Given the role of national language identity in parts of Asia, the task of language revitalization in Asia can be challenging.

2.5. Language situation in Europe

Europe is home to 284 living languages, of which 187 are safe and 97 are endangered (Lewis *et al.* 2013), and a further eight are listed as extinct (Whalen/Simons 2012) (see Graph 5).

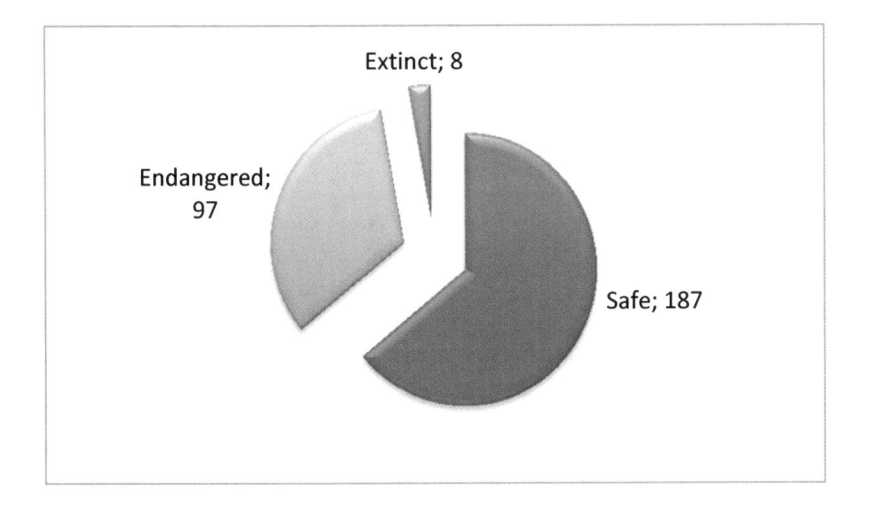

Graph 5. Language situation in Europe.

Stickel (2011) reports on European Union concern about the relationship between official national languages, and the regional and minority languages of Europe. This concern was articulated in the form of a European Charter for Regional or Minority Languages (Council of Europe 1992) which called on member states to eliminate any remaining restrictions in the use of regional or minority languages, with a particular call for the provision of education at the pre-school, primary and secondary levels in minority languages. There is also acknowledgement in the Charter for provision of teaching of history and culture related to minority groups. In this context, the minority language communities of Europe have, in many cases, a policy platform upon which to revitalize languages which have suffered decreasing numbers of speakers in the past.

Cenoz and Gorter (2008) report on the status of the following minority languages of Western Europe:

- Basque, a non-Indo-European language, has co-official language status in Spain. With 600,000 speakers, Basque is the main language of instruction in many schools in the Basque Autonomous Community.
- Catalan, a Romance language, has co-official language status in Spain. With 9 million speakers, Catalan is the main language of instruction in some schools in Catalonia.
- Irish, a Celtic language, is the national language of Ireland with a reported 1.66 million speakers, and is weakening.
- Welsh, a Celtic language, has official status in Wales. With 600,000 speakers, Welsh is increasingly used as the medium of instruction in schools in Wales.
- Frisian, a Germanic language, has second language status in the Netherlands. With 400,000 speakers, this is the weakest of the five minority languages of Western Europe described here.

Within Europe, the countries with the highest number of documented living languages are the Russian Federation, Italy and Germany. These are looked at in turn.

2.5.1. *Endangered languages of the Russian Federation*

The Russian Federation has 103 living languages, of which an estimated 51 are endangered. The languages of Russia include Uralic languages associated with the proto-Uralic people of the Ural Mountains. Speakers of this language family are now mostly found in northern Russia, Siberia and the Baltic region. Other languages of Russia are the Tungusic languages spoken in Siberia (as well as in north China), the Mongolic languages including Buriat spoken in southern Siberia and Kalmyk spoken along the Caspian Sea, and the languages of the Caucasus including over forty spoken languages in three family groups: Kartvelian, Abkhaz-Adyghean, and Nakh-Dagestanian (Matthews/Polinsky 2003).

Grenoble (2003) documents the effect of the use of Russian by non-Russian speakers as a process of Russification. By the 1970s, Russian had become the primary, and in many instances sole language of instruction for non-Russian children. The use of minority languages in school was increasingly marginalized. By 1994, most languages in the north of Russia had been replaced by Russian in schools and the workplace with the exception of Todhzin (a Tuvin dialect) where 85.5% of children were recently reported to be using their heritage language in school. In the case of Oroch, Sámi, Gilyak, Itelmen, and Mansi, nearly all children have adopted Russian as the language in the home.

Russian migration has shaped the language situation in the Krasno-Selkup Area between the Khanty-Mansi Autonomous Region to the south and the Krasnoyar territory to the east. In the area, five languages are spoken:

- Selkup
- Khanty
- Evenki
- Ket
- Nenets

In the 1970s, the ethnic Selkup made up 50% of the population. By the late 1990s, the population had tripled with Russian migration, and the Selkup found themselves outnumbered by Russians 3:1. In the 1980s, Selkup was introduced to primary school where children are learning the language as a second language, not a mother tongue.

The endangered languages of Russia include the following five most critically endangered languages, with the most recent estimate of remaining number of native speakers provided (sourced from Lewis *et al.* 2013):

- Bohtan Neo-Aramaic (nearly extinct)
- Hinukh (5)
- Kerek (no known native speakers)

- Sámi, Akkala (no known native speakers)
- Yugh (1)

2.5.2. Endangered languages of Italy

Italy has 36 living languages, of which an estimated seven are endangered. Italian, a romance language, linguistically dominates Italy. In addition to Italian, Rhaeto-Romance languages can be found in the Italian Alps (Matthews/Polinsky 2003).

The endangered languages of Italy include the following two most critically endangered languages, with the most recent estimate of remaining number of native speakers provided (sourced from Lewis *et al.* 2013):

- Emilian (no known native speakers)
- Romagnol (no known native speakers)

2.5.3. Endangered languages of Germany

Germany has 27 living languages, of which an estimated five are endangered. Germany is home to Germanic languages, including German and Frisian. In addition, Sorbian, a Slavic language, is spoken in an isolated part of Germany (Matthews/Polinsky 2003).

The five endangered languages of Germany, with the most recent estimate of remaining number of native speakers provided (sourced from Lewis *et al.* 2013), are:

- Frisian, Eastern (2,000 in Germany)
- Frisian, Northern (10,000)
- Saterfriesisch (1,000)
- Sorbian, Lower (6,670 in Germany)
- Yiddish, Western (5,000 in Germany)

The efforts of European Union members, and other countries in Europe, to embrace their regional and minority languages (see Stickel

2011) provide an opportunity for revival of endangered languages of Europe. However, the success of such a revival is dependent on the presence of a critical mass of people identifying strongly with the language, and a community committed to using the language in various domains including the home, school and public gatherings. In some cases, this may require language shift towards the minority languages, and an associated identity shift.

2.6. Language situation in the Pacific

The Pacific is home to 1,311 living languages, of which 873 are safe and 438 are endangered (Lewis *et al.* 2013), and a further 128 are listed as extinct (Whalen/Simons 2012) (see Graph 6).

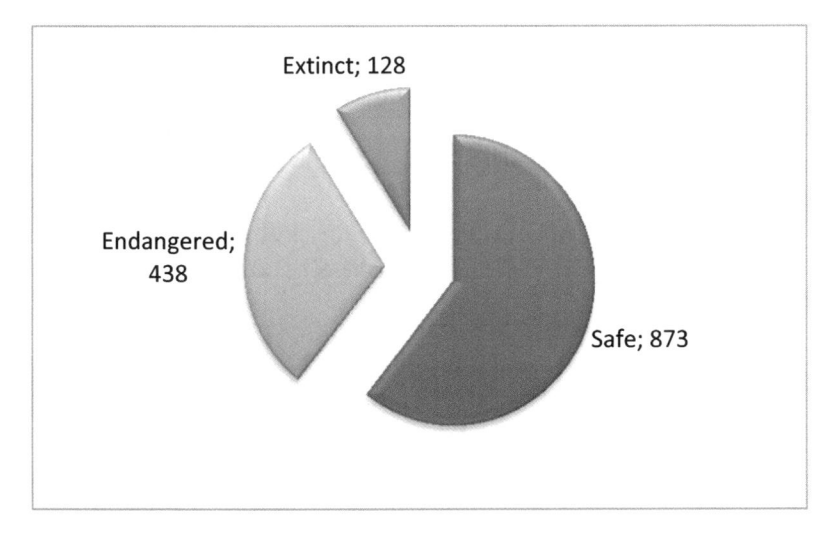

Graph 6. Language situation in the Pacific.

Tryon (2006) reports that the main pidgin and creole languages of the Pacific are Tok Pisin, Solomons Pijin, Bislama, and Hawai'i Pidgin.

These are used as lingua francas alongside English and French. In the case of Fiji, the British Colonial Government in Fiji selected one local language for communication and administration from 300 spoken dialects. In Vanuatu and the Solomon Islands, plantation labor resulted in language death. In Vanuatu, for example, Aore died and Araki became endangered.

Urbanization, and the search for improved economic opportunities, was the greatest threat to language vitality in parts of the Pacific. After independence, Pacific nation states used language for nation building. This was particularly the case in Melanesia. Vanuatu lacked a language to unite its people at the time of independence in 1980. The nearest to a common language was Bislama, an English-based pidgin, commonly used among ni-Vanuatu. Since independence, Bislama became the national and dominant language of Vanuatu.

Intermarriage in the Pacific has led to language shift in the next generation, particularly in Melanesia, but also in Tahiti, where children of mixed Tahitian-French parents typically speak French in the home, rather than Tahitian.

Crowley (1999) points to the attitude of European missionaries in the Pacific towards indigenous cultures and languages, with efforts made by missionaries in the past to modify local languages for the teaching of religious ideas. This process included selection of particular languages to develop written forms for religious purposes. This was particularly evident in Melanesia, creating local lingua francas.

Within the Pacific, the countries with the highest number of documented living languages are Papua New Guinea, Australia and Vanuatu. These countries will be looked at in turn.

2.6.1 Endangered languages of Papua New Guinea

Papua New Guinea has 836 living languages, of which an estimated 139 are endangered. Papua New Guinea is dominated by the Papuan languages, of which Enga has the largest number of speakers (157,000). The absence of centralized political power, standardization of language, or a writing system or literacy tradition did not allow any one language to become dominant. It is believed that the desire for distinctiveness in identity between neighboring groups in Papua New Guinea explains the vast diversity of languages found in the country where inter-group trading and commerce has been commonplace over the centuries (Plinsky/Smith 2003).

The endangered languages of Papua New Guinea include the following eight most critically endangered languages, with the most recent estimate of remaining number of native speakers provided (sourced from Lewis *et al.* 2013):

- Abaga (5)
- Kamasa (7)
- Kawacha (12)
- Labu (unknown)
- Momare (no known native speakers)
- Rema (unknown; nearly extinct)
- Turumsa (5)
- Unubahe (7)

2.6.2. Endangered languages of Australia

Australia has 214 living languages, of which an estimated 178 are endangered. Australia has been inhabited by indigenous groups for at least 50,000 years and developed over 250 different languages. Inter-tribal/national contact meant indigenous Australians were multilingual. The languages of Australia are not closely related to languages found outside the continent. They form two major groups: Pama-Nyungan and non-Pama-Nyungan. The Torres Strait Island languages found on the islands in the Torres Strait between Australia and Papua New Guinea include Kala Lagaw Ya, Meriam Mer, and Blaikman Tok (Austin 2003).

Evans (2007) reports that all indigenous languages of Australia are related at a distant level. The hunter-gatherer communities which populated Australia had between 50 and 5,000 speakers each, with between 1,000 and 3,000 being most common. While most languages of Australia have either died out or are severely endangered, small numbers remain in comparatively good health. These include, with estimated number of speakers in brackets:

- Walpiri (3,000)
- Arrernte (3,000)
- Western Desert (or Wati) (4,000)
- Yolngu-Matha (2,500)
- Kala Kawaw Ya (3,000)
- Wik Mungkan (1,000)
- Nyangumarta (700-800)
- Thaayorre (500)
- Tiwi (1,400)
- Anindilyakwa (1,000)
- Murrinhpatha (2,000)
- Bininj Gun-wok (1,500)
- Burarra (400-600)
- Ndjébbana (200)

Several pidgins and creoles related to English have developed in northern areas of Australia.

The endangered languages of Australia include the following 35 most critically endangered languages, with the most recent estimate of remaining number of native speakers provided (sourced from Lewis *et al.* 2013):

- Amurdak (1)
- Awabakal (no known native speakers)
- Biri (no known native speakers)
- Broome Pearling Lugger Pidgin (no known native speakers)
- Darkinyung (a few speakers reported in 2008)
- Daungwurrung (no known native speakers)
- Dhungaloo (no known native speakers)
- Dieri (no known native speakers)
- Gabi-Gabi (no known native speakers)
- Ganggalida (1)
- Gugu Badhun (no known native speakers)

- Gureng Gureng (no known native speakers)
- Karenggapa (no known native speakers)
- Karuwali (no known native speakers)
- Margu (1)
- Ngandi (no known native speakers)
- Nhanda (a few speakers reported in 1995; nearly extinct)
- Tagalaka (1)
- Umiida (no known native speakers)
- Unggumi (no known native speakers)
- Wadi Wadi (unknown; nearly extinct)
- Waka Waka (no known native speakers)
- Warungu (no known native speakers)
- Wulna (1)
- Yanda (few speakers reported in 2012)
- Yangman (no known native speakers)
- Yarluyandi (unknown; nearly extinct)
- Yatay (no known native speakers)
- Yawijibaya (no known native speakers)
- Yinwum (no known native speakers)
- Yirandali (unknown; nearly extinct)
- Yitha Yitha (no known native speakers)
- Yorta Yorta (no known native speakers)
- Yugul (unknown; nearly extinct)
- Yuyu (no known native speakers)

2.6.3. Endangered languages of Vanuatu

Vanuatu has 116 living languages, of which an estimated 55 are endangered. The languages of Vanuatu are predominantly Austronesian, distinct from the mainly Papuan languages of Papua New Guinea. Bislama, the pidgin of Vanuatu, is now firmly established in Vanuatu, providing unity across different language speakers (Plinsky/Smith 2003).

The endangered languages of Vanuatu include the following five most critically endangered languages, with the most recent estimate of remaining number of native speakers provided (sourced from Lewis *et al.* 2013):

- Araki (8)
- Lemerig (2)
- Nasarian (5)
- Olrat (5)
- Ura (6)

Crowley (1999) reports that, in the Pacific, speakers outside Australia do not, for the most part, regard their languages as endangered, despite language shift taking place in the Pacific. While the complacency towards language endangerment in Vanuatu, for example, is leading some linguists towards the view that their primary task should be documentation of the endangered languages before they become extinct, Crowley (1999) sees signs that the languages of Melanesia, Micronesia and Polynesia may still be healthy, for the large part, a century from now. The same cannot be said for many of the indigenous languages of Australia.

2.7. Summary

The data on endangered languages presented in the previous pages capture the situation in a range of regions. Reporting on the endangered languages of all countries and territories would add tremendously to the length of the book. Suffice to say that absent from the reporting in this chapter are many other countries with significant numbers of endangered languages.

When a language appears in a list of endangered languages followed by an estimated number of remaining native speakers in brackets, little is indicated about the speakers, their attitude to the language, and whether the language is increasing in strength, stable, or in decline. The reporting in this chapter focuses on many languages which are experiencing a significant decline in vitality over time. This may be in terms of low rates of transmission of the language to children. It may be in terms of decline in the use of the language in the community. It may be in terms of the average age of its few remaining speakers, signaling possible extinction in the near future. Quite a number of the languages listed may have no remaining fluent speakers, be they native speakers or second language users.

There are also languages listed which may be able to regain vitality. Reporting in 20 years from now may provide an indication of the extent of language revival, language shift and language loss.

3. Endangered languages

Krauss wrote in 1992 of the status of indigenous Alaskan languages. The report was grim. Ainu was thought to be extinct, and many other languages were critically endangered. Eyak was assumed to be next to be lost with only two remaining fluent speakers at the time, both elderly, followed closely by Ubykh, Iowa, Osage, Mandan, Abenaki-Penobscot, Yokuts, Coeur d'Alene, Tuscarora and Menomini. A feature of these dying languages was small numbers of remaining speakers, all aged, and no passing on of the language to younger generations.

Intergenerational transmission, the passing of language knowledge and use from one generation to the next, was reported at the time to be evident in only two of the 20 indigenous languages of Alaska (Yup'ik, Siberian Yup'ik of St. Lawrence Island) where children were still learning the language of their ancestors.

Basing his estimates on the reported number of languages and known intergenerational transmission, Krauss estimated that around 3,000 (or 50%) of the world's known 6,000 languages were not being satisfactorily passed onto future generations, and were likely to be lost.

Nettle and Romaine stress that "a language is not a self-sustaining entity" (2000: 5). A language's vitality can be measured in the vitality of use among the youngest generation. Some languages may have small numbers of speakers but display strength in transfer to younger members of the community and in the domains of language use. Other languages may have large numbers of speakers but be experiencing language shift towards more dominant languages. Thus, looking at numbers alone does not provide a clear picture of language vitality.

Barrena *et al.* (2006) identify two key factors in the vitality of languages. First, there is the degree of official status afforded to the language, either on a national or regional basis. There appears to be a relationship between the official status of a language and the attitude of the language users towards its vitality, with language decline associated with lack of status. Second, there is the pattern of familial transmission, whereby a language is passed from parents to children. A break in this transmission generates linguistic substitution, involving the replacement by children of the parental language with another language.

Barrena *et al.* (2006: 19) list a series of contributing factors to language decline:

- Danger to the speakers (war)
- Movement of the population (loss of land rights, deportation, migration)
- Economic or cultural subordination (colonization, influence of religion, cultural discrimination, assimilation)
- Direct linguistic discrimination (language repression)
- Negative attitudes towards the language

This chapter reports on endangered languages to highlight the type of communities affected, the types of threats to the language's survival, and the status of the language in each community of speakers.

3.1. Sign languages of North America

Davis (2010) indicates that North American indigenous sign languages emerged as a means of communication between speaking American indigenous groups as a lingua franca, as the alternative to a spoken language. They were also learned and used as a first language by deaf members of indigenous communities.

The Plains Indian Sign Language, as an example, was widely used until contact with Europeans. It was gradually replaced by English as a lingua franca towards the end of the 19th century. Today, the Plains Indian Sign Language is endangered, but still used by some indigenous groups for storytelling, rituals, legends, prayers, and conversational narratives. Plains Indian Sign Language is also used by some deaf individuals.

Another well-documented sign language of North America is Martha's Vineyard, widely used in Massachusetts between the 17th and 19th centuries. A form of English-sign bilingualism developed, used by hearing and deaf people, and transmitted to future generations. In the early 1800s, most deaf residents of Martha's Vineyard were attending the American schools for the deaf in Hartford, Connecticut. As deaf people picked up American Sign Language, Martha's Vineyard Sign Language became extinct.

3.2. Languages of Alaska

Krauss (2007) has identified the introduction of English-medium schooling as the trigger for language shift in many Alaskan indigenous language communities, whereby the mother tongue shifts from indigenous language to English over a period of five to ten years. Krauss talks of a cut-off age to mark this language shift above which almost all of a local population are native speakers, and below which almost none are. Further triggers for language shift among speakers of indigenous languages in Alaska have been urbanization (i.e., relocation from ancestral lands to urban centers, particularly Anchorage, Fairbanks, and Juneau), intermarriage, and dissociation from an ancestral community.

The effect has been a pattern of reducing numbers of native speakers of Alaskan indigenous languages over time, with over half Alaskan indigenous languages with less than 100 ageing speakers remaining. Eyak, an indigenous language within the Athabascan-Eyak-Tlingit language group spoken by the Eyak people who inhabited the Pacific Coast of Alaska, had one surviving native speaker in 2007, Marie Smith-Jones, aged 89. Sadly, today there are no remaining native speakers now to pass on the language.

Today, there is relative success with retention of indigenous language use among St Lawrence Island children (speakers of Siberian Yup'ik) and within sixteen villages where Yup'ik is widely spoken by children, and also with recent efforts to reverse language loss of Inupiaq among children.

3.3. Languages of South America

Campbell (2012) documents 420 languages spoken in South America, representing 108 language families, or roughly a quarter of the 420 known language families in the world. This includes, based on Campbell's data sources, 188 indigenous languages in Brazil, 65 in Colombia, 60 in Peru, 30 in Venezuela, 25 in Bolivia, and 15 in Argentina. Estimates of remaining languages of the Amazon Basin, the most linguistically diverse region of South America, vary between 240 and 300.

Crevels (2012) reports that the Bolivian Amazon basin was once home to an estimated 350,000 people grouped into an estimated 50 indigenous language groups within the Guapore-Mamore linguistic area, representing the Pano-Tacanan, Chapacuran, Arawakan, Tupian, Nambikwaran and Macro-Ge language families. This diverse linguistic area has suffered from linguistic loss since first contact with the outside world, to the extent that today possibly fewer than 20 of these languages are still spoken.

Recent census data suggest that some indigenous languages in Bolivia are seeing an increase in numbers of reported speakers, although this may be associated more with auto-identification with a language than knowledge of the language, in the context of land reform laws in Bolivia which have sought to reorganize land ownership along ethnic group lines. The reality is that over half of the indigenous languages in the Bolivian Amazon basin have fewer than 50 speakers.

In an effort to bring education to the indigenous peoples of the Bolivian Amazon Basin and to preserve their indigenous language use, Intercultural Bilingual Education (IBE) programs have been introduced to the region covering ten schools, with programs of language revitalization structured into the system. Since the year 2000, indigenous languages have been afforded official language status in Bolivia and their use can now be actively promoted in the educational system.

3.4. Languages of Thailand

Premsrirat (2007) identifies 70 languages of Thailand belonging to five language groups: Tai-Kadai, Austro-Asiatic, Hmong-Mien, Sino-Tibetan, and Austronesian. The 24 languages within the Tai-Kadai language group are spoken by 92% of the population, and include regional dialects of standard Thai. 20 Austro-Asiatic languages, all indigenous to Southeast Asia, are spoken by 4.3% of the population. 21 Sino-Tibetan languages, including 14 Tibeto-Burman languages spoken principally in the north and northwest of Thailand, and seven Chinese dialects spoken mainly in urban centers, are spoken by 3.1% of the population. Two Hmong-Mien languages (Hmong, Mien) are spoken by 0.3% of the population mainly in the north of Thailand. Three Austronesian languages (Patani Malay, Moklen, Urak Lawoi) are spoken by 0.3% of the population mainly in the south of Thailand.

Among the 70 languages of Thailand are a number of marginal languages found in border regions, including Tibeto-Burman languages (Karen, Lisu, Lahu, Akha) and Hmong-Mien languages (Hmong, Mien) spoken in the north and northwest, Austro-Asiatic languages (Khmu, Lua, Northern Khmer, Kuy, Mon), and Austronesian languages (Patani Malay). These marginal languages are spoken by people in neighboring countries representing a larger ethnolinguistic group, and serve as a lingua franca for the broader group of speakers.

There are also a number of enclave languages which are spoken by small, isolated groups, surrounded by more dominant language groups. These include Nyahkur, Chong, Kasong, Samre, So, Lawa, Bisu, Mpi, Moklen and Urak Lawoi.

3.5. Languages of Australia

McConvell and Thieberger (2006) report that, at the time of the first European settlement in New South Wales in 1788, 250 indigenous languages were spoken in Australia. Subsequent European settlement of the land, forced relocation of indigenous Australians to new lands, dislocation with the land and community and suppression of indigenous languages in schools resulted in variable patterns of language shift over time, with a tendency to replace the indigenous language with pidgin English or English, as the lingua franca. Some regions were affected more than others, depending on the duration and extent of European settlement in the area. The result is that, in the 1996 census, the proportion of the indigenous population speaking their traditional language was variable across Australia (p.59):

- Regions where more than 79% of the population are still using their heritage language: Arnhem Land, Central Australia and the Western Desert, a small part of Cape York Peninsula, the Torres Straits
- Regions where between 30% and 79% of the population are still using their heritage language: remainder of the Northern Territory, the north of Western Australia
- Regions where between 7% and 30% of the population are still using their heritage language: a few areas of western Australia, a large part of Southern Australia, most of Cape York Peninsula
- Regions where less than 7% of the population are still using their heritage language: Tasmania, Victoria, New South Wales, most of Queensland, southwest of Western Australia

McConvell and Thieberger (2006) report that, despite the language shift evident among indigenous Australian communities, identification with their heritage language remains important for most indigenous Australians, and many groups are keen to reclaim their heritage language.

3.6. Languages of Papua New Guinea

Papua New Guinea's language diversity has been attributed to a number of factors (see Sumbuk 2006: 93):

- Economic globalization which impacted negatively on minority languages in other parts of the world has not taken place in Papua New Guinea on a large scale. Thus, there has been relatively little economic incentive for language shift.
- The national constitution recognizes all languages as equal, including English and two pidgins, Tok Pisin and Hiri Motu.
- All languages are recognized as media of instruction in schools according to the National Literacy Policy.

In Papua New Guinea, the explanation for language diversity recognises that social contact between neighbouring groups has been widespread for centuries, and that bilingualism and multilingualism is similarly widespread. The explanation also recognises that there is no sense of dominance of one language over another. Small groups of speakers in Papua New Guinea have retained distinct language use as a symbol of pride, and as a mechanism of distinction. In other words, the more distinct the language, the stronger its potential value as a marker of group identity. This has resulted in resistance among neighbouring communities in Papua New Guinea to forces of language shift and assimilation which have been associated with communities in other parts of the world (see Sumbuk 2006).

Nevertheless, there are some developments in language use in Papua New Guinea which may result in greater language decline in future. First, English is being promoted as a language of education, governance, business and media communication. Second, there is an attraction to Tok Pisin as a symbol of English.

Sumbuk (2006: 86-87) indicates that data on the number of native speakers for each of Papua New Guinea's 860 indigenous languages are sketchy, as no specific data on native speakers are collected in the national census, and there has not been a linguistic survey of Papua New Guinea. What is known is that many languages of Papua New Guinea have survived for centuries with fewer than 100 speakers. In this part of the world, number of speakers does not reflect strongly on language vitality. Some languages of Papua New Guinea appear to have died out, or be close to extinction. These include Guranalum, Lae, Laua, Malkolkol, Ouma and Sene. In addition, Hermit and Kamasa may be extinct. This extinction could be the result of abandoning the language in favour of a more popular language. Such is the case with Tench, which is being abandoned by its speakers in favour of Musau, and with Malkolkol which is being abandoned in favour of Nakanai.

Sumbuk (2006: 89) reports on two languages of Papua New Guinea, Kaningara and Sare in the Blackwater Lake area of East Sepik Province, where Sare is spoken by 1,339 people spread across seven villages while Kaningara is spoken by 327 people in just one village situated in the same area. The two languages have survived side by side, with little borrowing evident between the languages. There is widespread contact between the two groups, and Kaningara speakers are conversant in Sare. Sare has not absorbed Kaningara for two main reasons. First, there is no attraction for Kaningara to Sare, as both groups share a common culture, with shared customs, beliefs and rituals. Second, the two groups proudly identify with their heritage language, and use the language difference to highlight their association with their respective community. In recent times, speakers of these two languages have been attracted to Tok Pisin, an English-based pidgin, but this lingua franca has not replaced the two languages. Thus, intergenerational transmission of the two local languages has remained uninterrupted over time.

3.7. Languages of Vanuatu

Vanuatu, located in one of the most linguistically diverse parts of the world, has been experiencing language loss over many decades. Reasons for past language loss are unclear, but more recent threats to language maintenance are urbanization (i.e., relocation to the urban centers of Port Vila and Luganville) and language shift to Bislama, which operates as a lingua franca in Vanuatu.

Tryon (2010) lists known extinct languages of Vanuatu for which little or no information is available except for memory of name of the language from the past. These include Gobon, Lalngetak, Odia, Ekarue, Niethro, Nokanoka, Latu, Mwe'ea, Sinie, Memie, Mbwere, Nggasai, Ral Aru, Ral Uri, Nivat, Natuaki, Utaha, Enyau and Novulamleg.

A further list of more recently extinct languages or languages on the brink of extinction includes Lemerig, Mwesen, Toula, Beleru, Netavu, Tavalpei, Vevatot, Moiso, Aje, Bot, Araki, Aore, Nethalp, Sowa, Hoti, Naati, Gara, Umbruul, Nitita, Viviti, Naman, Tape, Nese, Njav, Ningkira and Ura.

Tryon (2010) anticipates that an additional 20 to 30 languages of Vanuatu will face extinction in the coming decade. This includes languages currently with fewer than 100 remaining speakers, some of which are in close proximity to the urban centers of Port Vila and Luganville. This list of endangered languages includes Lehalrup, Mwesen, Mokoro, Wentuk, Ngen, Toksiki, Farafi, Farnanto, Atin, Redlahtur, Daruru, Moiso, Nioleien, Nevwol, Newoteyene, Nasvang-Farun, Nisvai-Vetbong and Bieria.

Vanuatu, Papua New Guinea and the Solomon Islands, represent one of the world's critical geographic areas for language protection due to high numbers of languages reported in the region.

3.8. Languages of Russia

Siberia covers a vast portion of the Russian Federation, occupying the land mass lying north of China, Mongolia and Kazakhstan. While the Russian language dominates to the West, in Siberia are found 25 local languages. Grenoble and Whaley (2006) report that seven local languages of Siberia have substantial numbers of speakers, including Buriat (318,000 speakers), Yakut (363,000 speakers), Tuvin (206,000 speakers), Altai (71,600 speakers), as well as Nenets, Dolgan and Evenki. The remaining 18 local languages of Siberia are critically endangered.

In Chukotka, in the northern part of the Russian Far East, indigenous Eskimo languages are no longer being passed onto children by their parents in a traditional manner. As an example, the Chaplinski Eskimos numbering around 900 have mixed population, and live alongside Chukchis, and newcomers to the area, mainly Russians and Ukrainians. The Chaplinski Eskimo language is today mainly spoken by the older generation, with some passive knowledge by younger people. Younger Chaplinski Eskimo speak Russian. In response to language shift away from the heritage language, there has been a program of teaching the Chaplinski Eskimo language in local schools, but a decreasing indigenous population is making this less effective. In spite of the poor language situation, the Chaplinski Eskimo retain a strong sense of identity and take pride in their cultural traditions (Vakhtin 1998).

3.9. Languages of the Cameroon-Nigeria borderland

The Adamawa Plateau region of Cameroon, bordering with Nigeria, is situated in a linguistically diverse region of the world. Griffiths and Robson (2010) provide insights into two linguistic groups within this region, the Wawa and Kwanja people. Both linguistic groups are facing threats to their linguistic and cultural way of life.

3.9.1. The Wawa

There are an estimated 2,500 Wawa speakers in total located in the township of Banyo and in thirteen neighbouring villages. The Wawa are multilingual, with most speaking Wawa and Fulfulde, the region's lingua franca. Many have knowledge of other local languages including Vute and Mambila. In addition, many know French through schooling, and some have knowledge of English. Those involved in commercial activities have knowledge of Hausa, which serves as a language of trade and commerce in the area. The Wawa are Muslims, and use Arabic in religious domains. Wawa has no written script, and Wawa children are taught to read in Arabic from the Koran.

Griffiths and Robson (2010) report that the Wawa have, so far, succeeded in maintaining their language through intergenerational transmission to children and widespread use in daily life. There is, however, a growing threat from Fulfulde, the local lingua franca, due to a process of assimilation of Wawa to the Fulbe way of life.

3.9.2. The Kwanja

There are an estimated 10,000 speakers of Kwanja located in twenty-five villages spread between Banyo on the Adamawa Plateau of Cameroon and Bankim on the Tikar Plain. There are three known dialects of Kwanja: Njanga, which has four remaining speakers in the village of Mbondjanga; Sundani, which has largely replaced Njanga and is used for Kwanja literacy; and Ndung, the most widely spoken Kwanja dialect.

3.9.3. Response to threats

The Wawa and the Kwanja people are subsistence farmers. Traditional practices including ancestor worship and sorcery are still evident among Kwanja, while the Wawa have assimilated more to the modern Fulbe way of life.

One long-term threat to Wawa and Kwanja language survival comes from the Fulbe culture and the Fulfulde language. The Fulbe are the largest ethnic group in the region, and were granted considerable political power by the German colonial authority which they continue to exercise until today. There has been a pattern of Fulbeization among local ethnic groups over the years, signifying adoption of a Fulbe identity, and corresponding abandonment of traditional practices, in an effort among minority groups to raise their social standing in the region. The Kwanja have established political and developmental organizations which have been effective in countering the Fulbe threat and maintaining Kwanja customs and practices. There has not been a similar effort among the Wawa.

Another long-term threat to Wawa and Kwanja language survival comes from the construction in the 1950s of the national route running from Yaounde, the capital of Cameroon, to the north of the country. The route runs through Kwanja and Wawa territory, and has increasingly exposed many Kwanja and Wawa to modern ways.

A third threat to Wawa and Kwanja language survival is access to education, and the use of French as the language of instruction in schools.

As a result of the various threats, the Wawa people have undergone a process of modernization in recent years, including abandonment of animist beliefs, a decline in hunting, dancing and traditional music, and adoption of modern technology including mobile phones. The process of change has affected culture and language. Wawa language served well as a means of communicating among hunter-gatherer communities. It has not served so well to communicate about modern concepts. Thus, there has been a shift away from Wawa to more favoured languages, particularly Fulfulde.

3.10. Languages of Brunei

Coluzzi (2010) documents the minority languages spoken in Brunei. These include eight Austronesian languages (Tutong, Belait, Dusun, Bisaya, Lun Bawang, Iban, Penan, Mukah), various Chinese varieties (Mandarin, Hakka, Hokkien, Cantonese, Hainanese, Teochew, and Foochow), and two dialects of Malay (Melayu Brunei and Kedayan). All the minority languages occupy the low position in a diglossic relationship with Malay. Thus, while the local language is used within villages among common speakers of the language, Malay is reported to be the preferred language at work, school, when shopping and visiting the doctor, and in contact with government officials.

3.10.1. Iban

One of the minority languages of Brunei, Iban, is also spoken in Sarawak and West Kalimantan. Coluzzi (2010) reports there are 700,000 Iban speakers in these three regions: 20,000 in Brunei, 660,000 in Sarawak (the largest ethnic group representing 30 percent of the whole population), and 11,000 in West Kalimantan.

3.10.2. Lun Bawang

Another of the minority languages of Brunei, Lun Bawang, is also spoken in northeastern Sarawak, Sabah and East Kalimantan. Coluzzi (2010) reports there are 62,000 Lun Bawang speakers: 1,000 in Brunei, 25,000 in Sarawak, 3,000 in Sabah, and 33,000 in Kalimantan.

3.10.3. Response to threats

The Iban and Lun Bawang are traditionally farmers, practicing the cultivation of a range of crops including rice, rearing animals, hunting and fishing. Their traditional beliefs were based on animistic and shamanistic elements. They once all lived in communal longhouses. While the Iban of Brunei largely continue to practice traditional beliefs and live in communal longhouses, the Lun Bawang living in Brunei have tended to adopt Christianity and now mostly live in nuclear family houses.

Coluzzi (2010) reports that, while both languages continue to be transmitted intergenerationally in Brunei, Iban is in a stronger position than Lun Bawang. Iban continues to be the preferred language for communication between speakers of the language. In contrast, a growing number of younger Lun Bawang speakers are reported to be shifting to the use of Malay as the preferred language of communication among their people. Nevertheless, attitudes to the language remain positive for both communities in Brunei, with evidence that both the Iban and Lun Bawang value and cherish their ancestral languages. While there is support across both language groups for official recognition of their languages, and expressions of hope that their languages will be taught at the local schools, there is greater acceptance among Iban than Lun Bawang for the heritage language assuming higher domain functions associated with use of the language in official communication and in the written media.

Overall, both groups remain optimistic (the Iban more so than the Lun Bawang) in the long-term vitality of their heritage language in the face of threats to continued use presented by Malay and English.

3.11. Toda language of Southern India

While the abandonment of a language signals loss in linguistic and cultural terms for the outside world, it may not always be viewed in these terms for insiders. de Swaan (2004) writes of parents who may be attracted to the language that will provide the greatest opportunities and open the most doors for their children. In the absence of a bilingual option, this may result in willing, if not enthusiastic, abandonment of the mother tongue. There may be cases where known bilingualism is disadvantageous on the labor market, in terms of perceptions and prejudices of employers, if the mother tongue is discriminated against.

Language abandonment can be the result of a rational desire for improvement among a language community. This is how Ladefoged (1992) explains the case of the community of approximately 1,000 Toda people of the Nilgiri Hills of southern India who speak Toda, a Dravidian language. The younger speakers of Toda have been consciously abandoning their language in an effort to be more fully involved in modern India. For the young Toda, there is an acceptance of the struggle that would be involved in trying to preserve their language. There is also a strong motivation to be linguistically a part of modern India. The younger Toda have chosen to focus on songs which are an important element of their religious life, as a symbol of their Toda language preservation and have shifted away from its use in daily communication. While the abandonment of Toda can be viewed in terms of linguistic and cultural loss of the language, for this community, the abandonment of Toda in daily life has been greeted in a more positive light.

de Swann (2004) examines the social setting of language to consider the effects of language loss on a community of speakers. He uses the term *language abandonment* to describe the process by which a community gradually stops using the language. de Swann suggests that the community may "use it less and less, start to neglect its finer points, resort increasingly to another, rival language, and eventually stop teaching the original language to their children and largely forget it themselves" (2004: 568).

The process of language abandonment may result from change within the community leading to higher value directed towards another language than towards the mother tongue. It may result from a preference for another language at school or other settings. It may result from domination by another people using another language.

The key point, though, is that the abandonment of a language is a complex process. It may be forced upon a language community or may be a result of a desire for change from within a language community. It may be viewed in a different light by different speakers, positively for some and negatively for others.

3.12. Summary

There are minority language communities facing pressure to assimilate into a more mainstream culture, and facing pressure to adopt a more widely used language. Some of these minority language communities respond to this pressure by looking to schools to maintain language use among younger generations, while some may be actively seeking to shift towards more dominant languages in the hope of securing better educational and employment opportunities for the younger generation.

Linguists working in this area need to be sensitive to the needs and aspirations of the language owners and users. There is, nevertheless, a responsibility to educate language users about the scope for maintaining a local language and adopting other languages, through multilingual models. The home needs to be identified as an important domain to continue the use of the heritage language. The school would be a domain suitable for bilingual or multilingual approaches to learning. There is, thus, a role for linguists in guiding with appropriate responses to language contact, language competition, and desires of people to be part of economic development.

4. Language policy

The colonial era represented a devastating period for many of the world's indigenous languages, due to the dominance of the colonial powers militarily, technologically, economically, and culturally. Well into the 20th century, suppression of minority languages was common practice at the government level, and the aftermath of policies and practices discriminating against minority groups is still evident in some parts of the world.

Language policy is the synthesis of beliefs and ideologies, intervention and modifications, and practice (see Spolsky 2004). The beliefs and ideologies regarding a language relate to the community of speakers, to society, and to the country's governing bodies. Intervention and modification relate to processes which impact on the language, its status, and the domains where it is used. Practice reflects what occurs, given the opportunities and constraints, in terms of language use. Language policy can promote or can restrict heritage language use. How people feel about the language, interventions enacted, and actual practices all impact on language survival.

The determination of a group of linguists to draft frameworks or declarations on language diversity and recognition of heritage and indigenous languages is important, but does not automatically lead to changes at the state or local level in terms of language policy. Declarations at the international level are non-binding in the sense that their intent cannot be imposed on member states. Thus, considerable responsibility sits with state government bodies to respond fairly and without discrimination to the linguistic diversity within their state borders. There is a challenge presented to nation states with diverse national or language groups residing within their territory to address nationalist desires for stability and shared purpose, to address needs for a common language within the country or at regional levels, and to address the rights of individuals and communities to use their language in the home, to be able to teach and use their language in school, and to receive recognition at the state or regional level of the value and significance of the language. Some countries are doing a better job than others in responding to these various concerns.

4.1. Suppression of indigenous languages

4.1.1. American indigenous languages

Crawford (2000) reports that the US government in the 1880s hired bounty hunters to round up indigenous American children and deliver them to boarding homes where English-only was spoken. A policy of banning indigenous languages, tribal religious practices, and ceremonies in the schools was enacted.

English was associated with 'civilizing' indigenous Americans. This belief continued through to the 1960s, and led to negative attitudes towards indigenous languages. A policy of assimilation of the colonized led to language loss in North America since the arrival of the Europeans. Among the languages to die were:

- Mohican (in Wisconsin)
- Catawba (in South Carolina)
- Yana (in California)
- Natchez (in Louisiana)
- Mashpi (in Massachusetts)

In 1868, the US government enacted a plan to establish schools where children were required to use English. In the 1880s, boarding schools were established for indigenous American children with strict English only rules and a program to erase indigenous culture, customs, and identities. The coercive assimilation policy prompted a response of resistance and determination among indigenous Americans to the threat presented. In the end, it was modernization that put the greatest strain on local language use seeing local languages used in increasingly fewer domains such as in the home, for rituals and ceremonies.

4.1.2. Māori

New Zealand experienced a decline in the status of Māori language following the European settlement from the 1860s and the subsequent widespread use of English. During the colonial era through to the 1920s, the Māori language was not recognized for its role in maintaining the pride and identity of Māori people, and Māori language was officially discouraged in schools. Many Māori elders questioned its relevance in a European-dominated world and supported adoption of English among Māori children to encourage rapid assimilation of Māori-speaking children into mainstream European society. Māori children were punished for speaking their language at school and many Māori parents encouraged their children to learn English (see Benton 1989).

Despite the focus on speaking English in schools, the Māori language persisted in Māori communities through to the 1930s. Māori was the language in the home, the community and the church. The language was being passed on intergenerationally from parents and elders to children. Thus, Māori and English occupied separate domains; Māori in the home and community, and English in the school.

New Zealand's involvement in the Second World War saw social change in society that impacted on use of Māori. Māori began moving into urban areas in greater numbers in search of employment opportunities, and Māori changed from being predominantly rural to being predominantly urban.

This urbanization increased contact of Māori with the English language, resulting in a decline in the number of Māori speakers. By the early 1980s, less than 20% of Māori were regarded as native speakers, and suggestions were that Māori was not being passed on sufficiently from parents and elders to children to prevent further language loss in the future. The response was the Māori language revival movement.

4.2. International and regional declarations

At the international and regional level, there has been considerable effort by linguists, non-governmental organizations and interested parties to push for declarations on language rights. This section reports on the content of some of these declarations.

4.2.1. European Charter for Regional or Minority Languages

In 1992 in Strasbourg, member states of the Council of Europe drafted the European Charter for Regional or Minority Languages. The Charter (Council of Europe 1992) provided for the delivery of pre-school, primary, secondary, vocational and tertiary education in the relevant regional or minority language where there was sufficient demand. This document focused attention on the importance of providing education at all levels in minority or indigenous languages, whether this be as the medium of instruction, or as provision of opportunities for learning of these languages in schools and tertiary institutes.

4.2.2. The Universal Declaration of Linguistic Rights

The World Conference on Linguistic Rights was held in June 1996 in Barcelona, bringing together linguistics experts, representatives from non-governmental organizations and representatives from PEN Centers (associations of writers). The Conference signed the Universal Declaration of Linguistic Rights (1996) which was then submitted to UNESCO in the hope that it would become the starting point for global action. The Declaration viewed languages as expressions of collective identity and called for the right for all languages to receive official recognition, and for all languages and cultures to be taught at all levels of education, including pre-school, primary, secondary, technical and vocational, university, and adult education.

4.2.3. UNESCO Universal Declaration on Cultural Diversity

On 2 November 2001, UNESCO adopted the Universal Declaration on Cultural Diversity (2001). The Declaration had a particular focus on freedom of expression, media pluralism and multilingualism. The Declaration called for safeguarding the linguistic heritage of humanity, encouraging linguistic diversity, respecting and protecting traditional knowledge, in particular that of indigenous peoples, and recognizing the contribution of traditional knowledge to environmental protection and natural resource management.

The Declaration calls for respect to be afforded to the mother tongue, in the context of safeguarding linguistic heritage. Specific reference to traditional knowledge reflects a growing appreciation of the significance of ecological knowledge systems for indigenous groups and for the global community seeking to utilize natural resources in a more sustainable manner.

4.2.4. First Indigenous Women Summit of the Americas

Participants at the First Indigenous Women Summit of the Americas, on December 1-4, 2002 in Oaxaca, Mexico, sought to unite in the struggle to end oppression based on religion, gender and social ranking. At the same time, they sought to recapture their ancestral spiritualities. At the Summit, members resolved that (Marcos 2010: 49):

> [...] spirituality is an indivisible part of the community. It is a cosmic vision of life shared by everyone and wherein all beings are interrelated and complementary in their existence. Spirituality is a search for the equilibrium and harmony within ourselves as well as the other surrounding beings.

The Summit had a particular focus on issues of indigenous spirituality, seeing these as a means to respond to the concerns felt about the plight of indigenous women in the Americas.

4.2.5. United Nations Declaration of the Rights of Indigenous Peoples

The United Nations General Assembly adopted the United Nations Declaration on the Rights of Indigenous Peoples (2006). The Declaration was the result of 25 years of work, and called for indigenous peoples to have the right to transmit their language and culture to future generations, to establish and control their educational systems and institutions providing education in their own languages, to utilize their traditional medicines and health practices, and to maintain their distinctive spiritual relationship with their traditionally used lands.

The reaction to the Declaration was overly positive, although four nations, Australia, Canada, New Zealand and the US, were initially less favorable to parts of the wording; however, eventually these four nations showed their support. The Declaration was widely seen as an historic document for indigenous communities across the world.

The international and regional meetings discussed here are non-binding. At the nation state level, there is scope for more meaningful changes.

4.3. State language policy

This section focuses on the language policies of nation states to highlight the approach these countries are taking at the language policy level to take account of the role and importance of their indigenous and minority languages.

Spolsky (2004) highlights a long list of countries which are officially monolingual, yet respectful of minority languages. These include:

- Austria: German (+ linguistic minorities)
- Brazil: Portuguese (+ Indian native languages)

- Costa Rica: Spanish (+ national languages of native peoples)
- Indonesia: Bahasa Indonesia (+ respected regional languages)
- Mali: French (+ other national languages)
- Nepal: Nepali (+ local mother tongues)
- Poland: Polish (+ national and ethnic minority languages)
- Venezuela: Spanish (+ local languages)

Then, there are officially bilingual and multilingual countries, including:

- Afghanistan: Pushto, Dari
- Cameroon: French, English
- Canada: English, French
- Kenya: English, Kiswahili
- Rwanda: Kinyarwanda, French
- Sri Lanka: Sinhala, Tamil
- Switzerland: German, French, Italian, Romansch
- Vanuatu: Bislama, French, English

Thomason (2001) reports on language status in the following countries to highlight the complexity behind language policy:

- In Finland, Finnish and Swedish share official status while Sámi is neglected.
- In Canada, French and English have official status while the indigenous languages are neglected.
- In Namibia, English has had official status since independence although it is only spoken by 5% of the population. Since 1997, there has been an effort to stimulate literate environments in African languages.

Colonialism shaped language use in different ways. Errington (2008) reports that the British and French spread their languages in their colonial domains as symbols of civilization and as instruments of rule. Mastery of English or French was viewed by these colonial powers as a means to elevate colonial subjects to a higher state of taste, morals, even intellect. In contrast, Belgium and the Netherlands were inclined to work with local languages in their colonial domains. The Portuguese made use of Bahasa Melayu, a local Malay language typically written with an Arabic-based script, in their efforts to establish a standard form of Malay to homogenize and unify the Malay people. For the Portuguese, Malay was a symbol of power and an instrument of its institutions.

In Africa, combinations of colonial and African languages are widely used for administration and are afforded official status. 19 African countries have adopted English as their official language, 22 have adopted French, seven have adopted Arabic, five have adopted Portuguese and one has adopted Spanish. Amharic has been chosen as the official language in Ethiopia, Kiswahili in East Africa, Somali in Somalia and Chichewa in Malawi (see Lodhi 1993).

Tryon (2006) indicates that, following independence, the Pacific nation states used language for nation building. This was particularly the case in Melanesia. Vanuatu lacked a language to unite its people at the time of independence in 1980. The nearest to a common language was Bislama, an English-based pidgin, commonly used among ni-Vanuatu. Since independence, Bislama has become the national and dominant language. Other important pidgins and creole languages of the Pacific are Tok Pisin, Solomons Pijin and Hawai'i Pidgin.

In Southeast Asia, national languages have been promoted for nation building. This has been the case in Thailand, Laos, Vietnam, and Cambodia, although there has been some tolerance for linguistic diversity in these countries. In Myanmar, Burmese has been promoted through official policy although there are 135 recognized ethnic groups (see Bradley 2006).

4.3.1. India

Thomason (2001) indicates that, in India, Hindi has been the official national language since independence in 1947 although it was unknown to most Indians. The controversial goal was for Hindi to replace English as the main language by 1965 although this was not achieved. 15 Indian languages enjoy official status as the languages of India:

- Hindi (in Uttar Pradesh, Rajasthan, Himachal Pradesh, Madhya Pradesh, and Bihar)
- Urdu (in Jammu and Kashmir)
- Bengali (in West Bengal)
- Gujarati (in Gujarat)
- Marathi (in Maharashtra)
- Oriya (in Orissa)
- Punjabi (in Punjab)
- Kashmiri (in Kashmir)
- Assamese (in Assam)
- Telugu (in Andhra Pradesh)
- Sindhi (in Sindh)
- Tamil (in Tamil Nadu)
- Kannada (in Karnataka)
- Malayalam (in Kerala)
- Sanskrit (sacred language of Hinduism)

4.3.2. Indonesia

Hajek (2006) reports that, in Indonesia, government policy is placing considerable strain on local languages. The sole official language is Bahasa Indonesia. This language has been actively promoted as a unifying language with some success. In 1970, 40% of the population understood Bahasa Indonesia. This figure rose to 67% by 1990. The language shift was due in part to compulsory schooling where the medium of instruction was Bahasa Indonesia. Other factors include the role of media, transmigration with government backing, and restricted access to local languages in schools where the local population does not exceed one million speakers.

4.3.3. East Timor

Hajek (2006) reports that, in East Timor, Dili serves as the lingua franca alongside the national language, Portuguese. Indigenous languages appear to be surviving despite past social upheaval, dislocation, and war.

4.3.4. United States

Crawford (2000) reflects on the relative failure of bilingualism in the US following passing of the Bilingual Education Act, 1968. The Act was never well understood or well implemented, and is now being challenged. California voted in 1998 to eliminate most native language instruction in Californian schools.

There are some relative success stories of bilingualism involving indigenous languages in the US. In the Choctaw community of Southern Oklahoma, the percentage of school starters speaking Choctaw as their native language remains around 90% although English is widely used. The tribally controlled school system operates in English. A federally-funded bilingual program in the 1970s proved unpopular with the community and was terminated. Today, a diglossic situation has evolved among the Choctaw in which English is spoken in school and Choctaw is spoken in the home, in social communication, and ceremonies. This is one of the few indigenous American communities where teenagers still communicate among themselves in the heritage language. In the past, discrimination against the Choctaw prevented their children from attending schools and this helped retain their first language. A pattern of self-reliance and self-isolation restricted the attraction of English among the Choctaw.

4.3.5. Australia

Australia is facing a rapid loss of its indigenous languages. Troy and Walsh (2008) indicate that most indigenous languages of Australia can be regarded as endangered, with just 20 indigenous languages regarded as healthy from 250 documented spoken languages in 1788 at the time of first European contact. In the face of this reality, a National Indigenous Languages Policy of Australia (2009) was drafted which sought to address the following aims:

- National Attention: To bring national attention to Indigenous languages – the oldest surviving languages in the world – and the pressures they face;
- Critically Endangered Languages: Reinforce use of critically endangered Indigenous languages that are being only partly spoken to help prevent their decline in use and to maintain or extend their common, everyday use as much as possible;
- Strengthening Pride in Identity and Culture: To restore the use of rarely spoken or unspoken Indigenous languages to the extent that the current language environment allows;
- Supporting Indigenous Language Programs in Schools: To support and maintain the teaching and learning of Indigenous languages in Australian schools.

Within the Policy is recognition of the status of the 145 indigenous languages still spoken in Australia, 110 of which are critically endangered. There is recognition of the importance of indigenous education in schools, and discussion of the importance of education in English. There is discussion of language revitalization, and of bilingual education programs.

4.3.6. New Zealand

Benton (2007) indicated that the Māori language, indigenous to New Zealand, was officially recognized as the ancestral tongue of the Māori people in 1974, and gained official language status in 1987. The New Zealand Human Rights Commission Languages in Aotearoa New Zealand Te Waka a Reo - Statement on Language Policy (2009) provides for:

- The right to learn and use one's own language is an internationally recognised human right.
- New Zealand has a particular responsibility under the Treaty of Waitangi and international law to protect and promote te reo Māori as the indigenous language of New Zealand. It also has a special responsibility to protect and promote other languages that are indigenous to the New Zealand realm: Vagahau Niue, Gagana Tokelau, Cook Island Mäori, and New Zealand Sign. It has a regional responsibility as a Pacific nation to promote and protect other Pacific languages, particularly where significant proportions of their communities live in New Zealand.

The Statement makes specific mention of Te Reo Māori as the indigenous language of New Zealand, in addition to other languages of New Zealand including New Zealand Sign Language (or Te Reo Rotarota). The cultural, religious and language rights of New Zealand's minority groups are protected in the Policy.

4.3.7. South Africa

Crystal (2010) indicates that South Africa has since 1993 officially recognized the following languages:

- Afrikaans
- English
- Ndebele
- Sesotho sa Leboa
- Sesotho
- Swati
- Xitsonga
- Setswana
- Tscivenda
- Xhosa
- Zulu

There is a call for the development of these languages and the promotion of their use.

4.3.8. Thailand

Person (2011) indicates the Royal Institute of Thailand has been leading the way in addressing language policy concerns. Nevertheless, Thailand is widely regarded at government levels as a monolingual country, despite the presence of 70 minority language communities. Recent policy statements have acknowledged the right of individuals to use the mother tongue for intra-group communication, and their right to learn both their mother tongue and standard Thai at school. There is currently a government funded program to provide mother tongue-based bilingual and multilingual education in the deep south of the country to Patani Malay speaking children, where Patani Malay, Thai and English are taught in local schools. Some other minority languages including Chong are taught in local schools in other parts of the country, but there is much scope for increased use of schools to preserve the linguistic and cultural diversity of Thailand.

4.4. Summary

There is evidence reported in this chapter of intent within the international community and at the regional and nation state levels to provide leadership and direction with regard to responding positively to linguistic and cultural diversity. Concepts of recognition, rights, and collective identity dominate the declarations. There is acknowledgement of the importance of heritage languages, knowledge and beliefs. There is recognition of the importance of access to education in the heritage language.

The opportunities provided in language policy at the state level, to provide recognition and, in some cases, afford special status towards indigenous languages, are encouraging. Steps taken to protect and promote language diversity at the state level are important developments, given the corresponding access to funding and expertize that could be provided.

Turning opportunities into positive change at the individual language level requires a combination of local language action and, in some cases, expert linguistic support. University-based research institutes are assuming an important role in terms of language documentation, language attitude surveys, language revitalization programs, development of orthographic systems and development of children's literature in the heritage language for use in schools.

Funding of such research activities is not always adequate to meet the needs, particularly in regions with vast numbers of indigenous languages in need of support. There is, thus, much scope for increased efforts in the area of language revitalization. Attracting a younger generation of people, including members of heritage language communities, to gain appropriate training in language documentation and language revitalization would be an important step towards maintaining a research focus in this important area of ethnography. University programs offering studies in language and culture, in language education, and in indigenous issues can lead the way in the training of future researchers. Appropriate funding to encourage indigenous representations in the student cohort of such programs would be highly advantageous.

5. Language revitalization

There is immense linguistic diversity among the world's inhabitants, with 7,105 documented languages listed in the Ethnologue (Lewis *et al.* 2013). The prospects for a growing number of these languages are dim, with a pattern of elderly speakers not passing their knowledge onto younger generations. With the death of a language community's last remaining native speaker, another language dies, taking with it the cultural knowledge of a community embedded in the language.

In recent decades, an increasing number of endangered languages have been the focus of language revitalization programs, with variable outcomes. This chapter introduces the concept of language revitalization and its various threats, and reports on some language revitalization programs.

5.1. Saving languages

Grenoble and Whaley (2006) describe the nature of language revitalization programs, suggesting that number and distribution of speakers, the role of competing languages, community attitudes towards the target language, and government policies collectively impact on the vitality of a language. Also of importance are the domains in which the language is used. A language survey, indicating numbers of speakers, patterns of use and attitudes towards the language can provide much of the information needed to assess the need and scope for a language revitalization program. The following models for language revitalization are suggested:

- Total-immersion programs
- Partial-immersion or bilingual programs

- Teaching the local language as a second language in local schools
- Community-based programs situated in the community focusing on music, dance, and other aspects of cultural significance
- Master-apprentice programs where the language learner is paired up with a native speaking teacher
- Language reclamation where languages no longer spoken are revived

Krauss (1997) looks to patterns of language use in the population as a means to assess intergenerational transmission, the passing of language knowledge and use from one generation to the next. Key indicators include the age groups speaking the language, and whether the language is learned and spoken by younger generations. As soon as a new generation fails to learn or use the language, the path towards possible extinction has begun.

A critical domain for language learning, language use and language transmission is education. Decisions made at the education level have an impact on opportunities to learn and use the target language, and impact on the development of literacy in the language. More broadly, these decisions can have an impact on community attitudes towards the language.

Many of the world's languages lack a written form. School-based programs for these languages typically require the development of an orthographic system, often based on a widely used language in the community, region or country. Linguists play a central role in this orthographic development (see Ogilvie 2011), and would ideally work closely with language community experts to decide on the purpose and products of the orthographic development, and devise a suitable writing system.

Work in this area may be restricted to the development of dictionaries or documentation of certain domains of language use. The work may focus on literacy development in the target language, through the development of writing systems and accompanying literature and textbooks.

5.2. Threats to language revitalization

Whaley (2011) points to problems often associated with language revitalization programs that have an influence on their success. The first problem arises from a tendency for outside agents to identify a language revitalization program with one particular community of speakers, even when other potential communities exist. In doing so, there will naturally be communities more closely associated with the program and communities less associated. There may arise tensions among the target population in terms of access to expertise and funding. There may be disagreement about the goals of the revitalization program and the direction of change. There may be disagreement among the target population about the role of external organizations and experts.

The second problem associated with language revitalization programs arises from a tendency for outside agents to associate a language revitalization program with a single standardized language. A single language form may be imposed on communities traditionally using different languages or different forms of the target language. This prescribed language may erode the connection with local knowledge, local values, and local beliefs. The prescribed language may erode the connection of people with ancestors and the past. The prescribed language may erode cultural identity.

The third problem associated with language revitalization programs is associated with more attention placed on the language than the speakers. The tendency to document language (phonetic, morphological and grammatical structures) can detract from attention on language as a social practice. The tendency is thus to develop resources such as orthographic systems, dictionaries, readers, textbooks and other educational resources. This overlooks the causes of language loss and language shift. Language revitalization programs need to address the motives for language use, and focus on the social practice of language use. There needs to be attention placed on the domains for language use.

The fourth problem associated with language revitalization programs is the role of outsiders and their decision-making power. Disagreements about regulation of language knowledge may arise, and these reflect differing ideologies regarding the nature of language. While the outsider may view language ownership as universal, speakers of the language may view themselves as guardians of the language.

The process of identifying a community of speakers and a language for a language revitalization program, overlooking the social dimension of language use and overlooking local feelings regarding language ownership can create conflict and tensions which undermine the efforts to reverse patterns of language loss.

5.3. Bilingualism and multilingualism

To reverse previous patterns among minority groups of younger generations abandoning use of their first language, linguists with an interest in language revitalization have looked to school education programs as the context for language maintenance in the form of bilingual and multilingual education programs.

Ideas about multilingualism have changed with time as new studies and their insights come to light. Where governments once banned the use of indigenous languages in schools, government policy on education in many countries is today embracing multiple language knowledge, and a body of empirical evidence suggests that knowledge of multiple languages has a positive impact on educational outcomes.
Previous thinking that the addition of a language early in life will slow overall language development has been challenged over the past 50 years by studies suggesting the superiority of bilinguals over monolinguals in cognitive development (see Bialystok 2005; Peal/Lambert 1962).

There is a developing research interest in the nature of self-identity among bilingual students (see Benet-Martínez/Haritatos

2005). This builds on Berry's (1990) interest in how acculturating immigrants and ethnic minorities negotiate their identification with their culture of origin (i.e., retain the old identity) and with the dominant culture (i.e., adopt the new identity). This is a relatively under-researched area, although the expectations are that future research in this area will provide some guidelines on how schools and communities can assist local language background students with negotiating their identification with the minority (i.e., local) and majority (i.e., mainstream) languages and cultures.

Bilingualism or multilingualism can be seen as a response to the challenges presented by linguistic diversity. Through the provision of opportunities to learn and use more than one language at school, the heritage language and more dominant languages can be promoted. Through exposure in school to the heritage language, children can retain an important link to their people, their culture and their past, and can look forward to a future where the heritage language will play an important role in their lives. Through exposure to more dominant languages, children can have access to educational and vocational opportunities enjoyed by others. They will be able to participate in external examinations in the dominant language, and move out of their community if needed or desired, equipped with the linguistic resources to succeed in their pursuits.

The mode of education in the school can reflect the language situation of the target population. This mode could be immersion in the dominant (second) language at school, on the basis that the heritage (first) language is widely used in the home and in social interactions outside of school. In this way, both languages are developed and maintained in separate domains.

The mode could be dual language instruction, where the medium of instruction is divided between two languages. This is a form of teaching *through the language* rather than directly teaching the language. The mode could be mother tongue-based programs, where children are exposed to their heritage language in the initial years of schooling through a local native-speaking teacher. The dominant (second) language is then introduced in latter years, while the heritage language continues to be taught, adopting a bilingual mode of delivery. Other languages can be progressively introduced, including foreign languages.

In some contexts, the heritage language can be taught as a subject in local schools to accommodate the requirement of language policy for the dominant language to be the medium of instruction for the syllabus, as official or national education policy.

With each approach, the school is only one domain in the process. The home and community represent equally important domains for language use, and the modes of bilingual and multilingual education adopted need to take account of the complementary roles performed by family and friends in the home and community settings, and the school.

Where the heritage language is used as a medium of instruction, local paradigms of learning may be more appropriate to follow than paradigms used in mainstream education. This would reflect the view of language as expressions of self and group identity, and as repositions of knowledge (see Baker 2011). This approach to instruction using local paradigms of learning typically requires native-speaking teachers who are enthusiastic about embracing their heritage identity, and promoting identity awareness and development among children of heritage language background.

Baker (2011: 210) highlights these strong forms of bilingual education:

- Immersion: bilingual classes with an initial emphasis on the second language
- Maintenance of heritage language: bilingual classes with an emphasis on the first language
- Dual language: minority and majority languages used
- Mainstream bilingual: two majority languages used

School-based bilingual and multilingual educational programs are likely to play a role in shaping students' identities, with scope for both preserving students' identification with their home language and home culture, and allowing identification with the mainstream language and culture. Where collective identity within a community portrays a positive attitude towards use of the local language, the prospects for continuation of use of the language by future generations are likely to be enhanced. Ansaldo (2010) argues that, in bilingual and multilingual settings, there can be a process of identity alignment to include elements of multiple languages in use. This can be motivated by desires to retain the heritage language while adapting to the wider language environment to gain access to economic rewards.

The perceptions held by the wider community of the value and status of a specific language impact on an individual's self-view and identity formation. If children sense appreciation and respect for their local language from parents, schoolmates and teachers, there is likely to be a strong basis for children to embrace the language with pride, and develop their self-identity with a positive role for the local language, regardless of how many other languages are being learned and used.

5.4. Revival of indigenous languages

5.4.1. Hawaiian

Warner (2001) describes how the Hawaiian people thrived for 1,000 years after migrating to Hawaii in the 8th century. Their language, though unwritten, was a sophisticated store of knowledge and understanding about the natural environment, resource use and conservation, myths, histories and religion. Following the arrival of the European, the Hawaiian language began to be replaced by English in important domains such as commerce, government, religion and education. The first English medium school in Hawaii was established in 1839. In 1848, 99% of common schools were taught in the Hawaiian medium. In the early 1900s, no schools were taught through the medium of Hawaiian. Hawaiians, at this time, began replacing Hawaiian with Hawai'i Creole, a local pidgin.

In the late 1960s, Hawaiians became interested in reviving their language and culture, and Hawaiian became the official native language of the state of Hawaii in 1978. At that time, there were an estimated 2,000 native speakers of Hawaiian. In 1984, following in the footsteps of the Māori revival movement in New Zealand, the first of the Punana Leo (language nest) total immersion preschools were opened in Hawaii. By 1999, eleven Punana Leo catered for a student population of 2,009. The Papahana Kaiapuni Hawai'i (Hawaiian Language Immersion Program) catered for children from the Punana Leo who wished to continue in Hawaiian medium education at primary and secondary school levels.

5.4.2. Te Reo Māori

According to Benton (2007), literacy among the Māori was widespread in early colonial times in New Zealand, partly through Christian church-run Māori-medium primary schools from 1814. Until the 1940s, though, secondary schooling was largely out of reach to the Māori, particularly to those in isolated rural communities. The Native Schools Act 1858 required that the curriculum include the ordinary subjects of primary English education. There was a widely held view among administrators at the time that schools could turn Māori children into English people in terms of language, manners, and morals.

In 1867, a national system of village day schools in Māori-speaking communities was established with the aim of facilitating the teaching of English language and English ways. In the 1880s, teachers were encouraged to use the Māori language as a bridge to English. By the 1900s, compulsory schooling in New Zealand banned the use of Māori in native schools and in the school grounds. Some Māori leaders led a boycott of schools to resist cultural and linguistic shift promoted by the colonial government. This localized resistance faded by the 1930s, although suspicion of the schools remained. The policy led to negative attitudes towards the Māori language.

Many Māori parents had, since the 19th century, viewed the knowledge of English as essential for the Māori to overcome disadvantage and regain economic and political parity with the British colonial power. Māori language was still widely used in Māori villages at this time, and was being successfully passed onto younger generations of Māori. Up to the 1960s, the Māori language remained central to Māori identity and distinctiveness.

After its peak in 1950, the Māori language started to fall into decline, due largely to urbanization of rural Māori. By the 1970s, there were a dwindling number of Māori communities and English was fast becoming the dominant language in Māori homes. At this time, it became clear to many Māori elders that the loss of Māori was detrimental to Māori self-determination, and a Māori revival movement was born.

In 1976, a bilingual school was set up in Ruatoki. The Ataarangi movement was also set up around this time in which the Māori language was shared between native speakers and learners. In 1982, the Kohanga reo movement was formed in which voluntary Māori-medium preschools were established in urban and rural areas. The number of these schools grew rapidly from 5 in 1982 to nearly 400 by 1985. There was also an increased use of Māori in state schools to reflect growing demand, in addition to setting up of new bilingual schools. Other school-based programs followed, including:

- Kura Kaupapa Māori (primary schools where Māori is the medium of instruction with Māori paradigms of learning)
- Wharekura (Māori-medium secondary schools)
- Wānanga (state Māori-medium higher education institutions).

Today, official language status is afforded in New Zealand to Te Reo Māori alongside English and New Zealand Sign Language, as part of a broader program of Māori language revival (see J. King 2001).

The relative success of the Māori language revival program is due in large part to the cultural pride, determination and collective spirit of Māori elders to combat a pattern of language loss. The attribute of pride in one's language and culture, and the determination to work towards language maintenance and revival may be the key to success with other language revitalization programs. Although research institute support and supportive educational policies have been seen to facilitate positive change (see, e.g., Premsrirat 2007), without a local community providing continuity of leadership and commitment, success of a language revitalization program may be limited at best.

In the case of Māori, a substantial population base and the absence of competing indigenous languages may have helped in developing revitalization programs across the country and across educational sectors (pre-school, primary, secondary, tertiary).

5.4.3. Languages of Thailand

Thailand is a linguistically diverse country with 70 spoken languages in use. Many of these languages lack a written script. The historic use of standard Thai as the language of instruction in schools, the widespread use of the four regional dialects (Northern Thai, Northeastern Thai, Central Thai and Southern Thai), and the increasing importance attached to teaching of English language in schools represent challenges to the survival of local languages in Thailand.

Until recently, educational policy in Thailand has not specifically focused on preservation of the use of local languages. The result has been a pattern of decreasing use of many languages over time, bringing some to the verge of extinction.

Recent efforts in Thailand have been devoted to reversing a national trend of language loss over time, mirroring an increasing appreciation globally of linguistic and cultural diversity. Thai universities have partnered with local community groups to confront the challenge of preserving some of Thailand's local languages (see Premsrirat 2007). In addition, current educational policy in Thailand provides room in the curriculum to teach local content, including the local languages, alongside the mainstream syllabus.

There has been a particular interest in Thailand in mother tongue-based approaches to language preservation through which students are first exposed in school to their heritage language by native-speaking teachers, before the gradual introduction of standard Thai, and then possibly other languages (e.g., English). The mother tongue-based bilingual and multilingual education programs have required development of written scripts for languages lacking one, with a preference for use of Thai characters. This has enabled written documentation of languages, development of dictionaries, and preparation of books and other educational resources for use in schools.

The hope and expectation is that children will be more likely to engage with their studies at school and attain good educational outcomes if they enter primary schools where their mother tongue is widely used and accepted, and then gradually are introduced to the national language (i.e., Thai), and then possibly other languages such as English. The thinking is that the respect attached to home languages in school settings may promote positive senses of identity and pride among children from language backgrounds other than Thai, and this positive sense of identity may help promote positive attitudes to learning. Data gathered in the coming years from existing programs of this type will indicate the extent to which the hopes are realized and expectations met.

One language, standard Thai, has served to unite the Thai people. This language is given official status as the national language, and serves as the medium of communication in all levels of Thai society. The Thai language is part of the Chinese-Thai branch of the Sino-Tibetan family of languages, and has its origins with early Thai settlers to Thailand. Evidence of a well-developed written form of the language appears on a stone tablet dating back 730 years to 1283 CE, during the reign of King Ramkamhaeng during the Sukhothai period of Thai history.

In the following century, Buddhist texts written in Thai script began to emerge. The success of Thailand in resisting colonization by the major European powers and ensuring the continuity of Thai rule over the Kingdom has ensured the continuity of use of the Thai language at all levels of government, education, commerce and in the media. In addition to Standard Thai, four regional dialects of Thai/Lao are widely used in Thailand: Northern Thai (or Kammuang), Northeastern Thai (or Lao Isan), Central Thai (or Thai Klang), and Southern Thai (or Paktay). In addition, 20 lesser-used dialects/languages within the Tai language group are spoken.

Successive generations of well-educated young Thais have studied abroad, principally in Europe, with the more recent addition of

North America, Australia, New Zealand and neighboring countries. In addition, foreign language teaching is a core element in the Thai school curriculum. Thus, there is a history of foreign language teaching and learning among Thais.

The emergence of English as a language of international communication over the past decades has seen a corresponding steady rise in the role of English in the Thai education system. With the support of successive Thai governments, schools and universities have increasingly offered a range of English only and Thai-English programs to cater for expatriate and Thai students.

The recent rise in the status of English alongside Thai in the Thai education system represents a challenge to those seeking to preserve local language use. A response to this challenge has been the development of bilingual and multilingual models of teaching and learning which incorporate local languages.

There are 70 documented languages of Thailand. These can be represented as five language groups:

- Austro-Asiatic (23 languages)
- Austronesian (three languages)
- Sino-Tibetan (18 languages)
- Hmong-Mien (two languages)
- Tai (24 languages/dialects)

Among these 70 languages, Premsrirat (2007) has identified fourteen which are severely endangered: Bisu, Chong, Chung, Kasong, Lawa, Lua, Mlabri, Moklen, Mpi, Nyahkur, Sakai, Samre, So and Urak Lawoi.

Bisu, within the Sino-Tibetan language family, is an example of an enclave language under threat. Person (2005) has documented the status of the Bisu language spoken by fewer than 1,000 people in two villages in Chiang Rai province in northern Thailand. Aside from the speakers of Bisu in Thailand, there are Bisu speakers in Yunnan province, China, from where the Thai Bisu emigrated in the early 19th century. There is as yet no known contact between the Thai and Yunnan Bisu groups.

Person (2005) indicates that in the two Bisu villages in Thailand, Bisu is widely used in the home, in the village community, and in the fields. The Bisu have, over the years, adopted Northern Thai as a contact language with non-Bisu people, and children acquire both Bisu and Northern Thai from birth. Northern Thai is widely used at school and to discuss matters of education. School-aged Bisu also learn Standard Thai through schooling, and many are confident in Bisu, Northern Thai and Standard Thai.

As a literacy development project, specialists from a local university have assisted in the development of a written script for Bisu based on Thai characters, and the development of the first Bisu books. There remains concern, though, about the future of Bisu and other enclave languages in Thailand, as exposure to other languages challenges local efforts to pass the heritage language onto each new generation.

The Research Institute for Languages and Cultures of Asia, Mahidol University, is one of several research centers in Thailand involved in programs to document and revitalize languages in Thailand. Programs include surveys of language use, development of orthographic systems based on Thai characters, development of dictionaries, children's books and educational resources, and community projects such as recording of traditional knowledge in the local language. Where feasible, programs of teaching local languages in schools as a subject by native speakers have been promoted to ensure continuity of language knowledge through to future generations.

A particular focus of the research institute's activities has been mother tongue-based approaches to bilingual and multilingual education, in which students receive instruction in their mother tongue in the first years of school, with the gradual introduction of Thai and then possibly other languages (such as English) in later stages. There is an important role for heritage language-speaking teachers in such programs.

In 2007, the Patani-Malay mother tongue-based bilingual/multilingual education program began, with Grade One students commencing the program in 2008, hence completing Grade Six in 2013. This program caters for Patani-Malay speaking children in

Thailand's southern provinces of Satun, Patani, Yala and Narathiwat. A distinguishing feature of these four provinces is the widespread use of Patani-Malay, a language within the Austronesian family group, by an estimated 83% of its predominantly Muslim population, giving these four provinces a distinctive language and culture within mainstream Thai society. Yearly assessments of these students are providing an evidential basis for assessing the feasibility of this approach to language maintenance and revitalization.

The Patani-Malay mother tongue-based bilingual/multilingual education program model follows steps from the first language (Patani-Malay) to the second language (Thai), and then to other languages (e.g., English) in an additive mode where the first language is retained through to the completion of primary schooling. Starting with the development of oral language skills in the first language (Patani-Malay) during the first semester of Kindergarten Year One, students then move on to learn the written form of Patani Malay in Kindergarten Year One, Semester Two, oral skills in the Thai in Kindergarten Year Two, and then the written form of Thai in Grade One to Grade Six. English is first introduced in its spoken form in Grade One, moving to include the written form of English from Grade Four. By Grade Six, students are working with the spoken and written forms of Patani-Malay, Thai and English.

The mother tongue-based bilingual or multilingual education programs appear to be a way forward in Thailand for language revitalization. These programs are reliant on strong community involvement, suitable teacher training programs, the development of educational materials (including the development of written scripts for languages lacking an orthographic system), and an evaluative component to assess the extent to which educational achievement and literacy levels in the target language meet expectations.

5.4.4. The Iquito dictionary project, Peruvian Amazonia

Beier and Lev (2006) brought together linguists, graduate students and native speakers of Iquito in a community-participatory project aimed at documenting the Iquito language in writing and developing written resources, whereby training of and capacity building among local native speakers enabled locals to be the main drivers for decisions about the project. There was a sense of urgency to the project as the last remaining 25 native speakers were all aged over 55, and 25 partial speakers were all aged over 30. The language was no longer being transmitted to younger generations. The project developed a dictionary, grammar, audio and visual resources, books and pedagogical materials.

5.4.5. Maintenance of Yi in Yunnan, China

All nationalities in China have a constitutional right to use and develop their own spoken and written languages, whereby a local standard language variety is identified to be promoted locally in terms of language and culture. There is also a policy of high level promotion of *Pǔtōnghuà* (or standard Chinese) throughout China. Within this context, there is variable success with minority language preservation among China's recognized 55 national minorities. Yi is one such nationality with its historical roots in Kunming, Yunnan.

Bradley and Bradley (2002) have documented the language policy and language maintenance of Yi in Yunnan. There are a reported 6.6 million ethnic Yi in China, four million of which reside in Yunnan province, making Yi the largest non-Han linguistic group in Yunnan.

Six regional Yi languages are spoken in Yunnan. In the 1980s, there was a focus on the development of a standardized script for Yi in Yunnan based on classical Yi characters. Subsequently, Yi language textbooks were prepared, based on this standardized script for use in primary schools.

Local efforts to promote use of Yi in schools have been frustrated by a pattern of reluctance on the part of teachers and administrators to disadvantage Yi children in an education system which favors knowledge of pǔtōnghuà over minority languages in terms of access to knowledge through textbooks, performance in provincial and national exams, and language status.

Bradley and Bradley (2002) look beyond efforts to preserve the use of Yi to reflect on the plight of other minority language groups in Yunnan Province which have not received the attention that has been afforded to Yi. The assumption is that Yunnan, once a linguistically and culturally diverse province, is rapidly losing its linguistic diversity as an undocumented number of local languages are not being passed onto future generations.

5.4.6. Revitalization of Quechua in Ecuador

Kendall King (2001) has documented programs to revitalize use of Quechua among the Saraguro people of southern Ecuador. The Saraguro people have experienced language shift away from Quechua towards Spanish that has been associated with increasing engagement with the outside world, and changing incentives and opportunities for the Saraguro to acquire Spanish. Language shift has been directly linked to recognition among the Saraguro of the importance of Spanish for participation in the market economy, including the trading of products such as rice, salt, sugar, and cheese, cattle sales, land transactions, and borrowing money. It has also been directly linked to humiliation and embarrassment associated with use of Quechua.

Starting in the 1950s and 1960s, Saraguro parents shifted from use of Quechua to use of Spanish as the contact language with their children. This shift was reinforced by local school policy at the time, which permitted instruction in and use of Spanish only in the local schools. Spanish became dominant in the Saraguro communities over a period of a few decades. Today, while older generations continue to speak Quechua and are essentially bilingual in Quechua and Spanish, younger generations have very limited knowledge of the heritage language, and are essentially monolingual in Spanish. Quechua is still used among the community elders for humor and for telling secrets. However, its use in the home is very limited.

Attitudes towards the pattern of language loss among the Saraguro are typically a combination of sadness, embarrassment and regret; the loss is seen as disrespectful to the elders and ancestors. Quechua provided a link with the past, and this link is being severed.

There is, indeed, a determination on the part of the Saraguro elders to preserve positive attitudes towards their indigenous culture. Increasingly, there is awareness of the importance of the language in the struggle to maintain ethnic identity among the Saraguro.

Since 1989, a policy of regional bilingual intercultural education has been implemented in the local schools. Local teachers, many of them Saraguro, talk of the importance of reverting to the use of Quechua in schools and the home. Quechua is now being taught in schools as a language. There is, however, some concern raised by Kendall King (2001) that the approach to teaching of Quechua in schools may not be sufficient to revive use of Quechua among young Saraguro.

5.4.7. Language revitalization in Australia

Walsh (2003) reports that, at the time of first contact between the indigenous Australians and the Europeans, there were an estimated 70 indigenous languages spoken in New South Wales. There has been a pattern of language loss over time. Language shift has resulted from forced and voluntary relocation from traditional lands, particularly movement from rural to urban areas. For indigenous Australians, language is linked to the land. In severing contact with the land, the links to the language may also be severed. Many indigenous Australians associate themselves with the languages of their parents and grandparents, resulting frequently in more than one linguistic association.

Following an initial assessment process which began in 1999, the focus of language revitalization in New South Wales has been on some key questions: Which languages should be revitalized? Who should teach the language and who should be taught? What should be the role of experts in the revitalization processes?

5.4.8. Welsh

Morgan (2001) reports on revitalization of the Welsh language in Wales. In 1955, a secondary school was established where history, geography, and religion, among other subjects, were taught through the medium of Welsh. The culture of the school administration and teaching was distinctly Welsh. Following this pioneering effort, Welsh medium education blossomed to include primary, and some secondary education for children of both Welsh and non-Welsh background.

A key to the success of the Welsh medium schools was that teachers were committed to reviving Welsh, and students benefitted greatly from this enthusiasm. By 1990, there were 553 nursery groups and 340 mother-and-toddler groups to cater for pre-schoolers. A census in 1991 indicated a considerable increase in the number of Welsh speakers in Cardiff and South Glamorgan over 1981 figures, reversing a pattern of language loss over the preceding 100 years.

5.4.9. California master-apprentice program

Hinton (2001) reports on a Master-Apprentice Language Learning Program in California set up in 1992 by the Native California Network. 20 different languages have been taught in the program, including:

- Karuk
- Hupa
- Wintuan
- Maidu
- Pomo (Central and Northern)
- Washo
- Mono
- Chukchansi
- Choinumni
- Wukchumni
- Fort Mojave
- Chemehuevi

- Kiliwa
- Kumeyaay
- Paiute

The master-apprentice methodology requires communication to take place in the target language only and includes a lot of visual aids, repetition and recall. The focus is more on oral language than written language. The use of recording devices is encouraged to minimize the amount of time and effort spent on the written language. The goal is that after three years, the apprentice will be conversationally proficient in the target language and ready to teach others.

5.5. The future of language revitalization

There is a possibility that other endangered languages will join the list of recently extinct languages alongside Eyak, with remaining native speakers reaching old age and no new generations of native speakers to ensure continuity of the language. There is also hope that many local languages will survive, with substantial numbers of speakers and school-based programs devoted to revitalization and preservation.

One key factor appears to be the degree of determination of a community of speakers to preserve their language in the face of challenges, and this determination appears to be linked to the degree of local pride in the language and culture. The sense of pride in one's language and culture is, to a large extent, shaped by the perception of others towards the language and culture. A positive attitude towards the language in the home is an important starting point. A positive attitude towards the language and culture in the local community and the local school appears critical to language continuity.

Arguably, if, at a national level, there is value attached to local languages and cultures, and resources directed at supporting their continuity, including through educational programs, it could be possible to ensure a geographic home for all languages, where native speakers sense the value attached to the language they know, and feel responsible for ensuring its continuity.

An important step towards raising the status of local languages could be to construct language maps at the regional level, whereby groups of speakers of the same language in different regions, isolated by time and geography, are able to make contact and share their resources, knowledge and spirit of self-determination. The less than 1,000 Bisu speakers in Thailand who share a language with the Bisu speakers in the Yunnan Province of China are an example of an enclave language community that could well benefit from this type of linguistic and cultural collaboration (see Person 2005). There are Bisu speakers in neighboring countries, and they could also benefit from this contact. Records of forced and voluntary migration could provide clues to assist with this language identification project.

6. Knowledge systems

Languages, in the view of Maffi (2002), serve as repositories of and transmission vehicles for traditional ecological knowledge. This view of languages reflects the realization that societies inhabiting a land will, with sufficient time and continuity of presence, assume knowledge of their environment based on the effect of human presence. Some communities, through trial and error, may evolve practices in which resources can be harvested in sustainable ways. Some may construct detailed knowledge of seasonal changes and weather patterns, of changes to the landscape, and changes to plant and animal life. Some may document medicinal use of plants. Such knowledge can be passed from one generation to the next through oral traditions. Maffi views the loss of a language as also a loss of local knowledge, beliefs, values and practices.

Nettle and Romaine (2000) share this view of languages as sources of accumulated wisdom, with each language providing a different view onto the world reflecting the response a community of people have to their environment and their need to survive. Languages may die when traditional practices die out or are prohibited.

Traditional knowledge systems are associated with sustainable and adaptive natural resource management, in which local communities co-exist with the natural world by responding to environmental feedback and environmental change (see Berkes 1993; Berkes/Colding/Folke 2000; Ellis 2005).

Languages are seen as repositories for knowledge (see Baker 2011) in the sense that shared understandings within a community are transmitted through language. The shared understandings, developed and refined over time, are held in the lexicon of the language. Some cultures have evolved complex lexical representations relating to important aspects of daily and ritual life. These may relate to tidal or climatic patterns for coastal dwellers, or to snow and ice conditions for arctic dwellers. There may refer to traditional places of importance (i.e., place names). Through use of these names, people establish an important link to their land and their past. There may be terminology used for illnesses, and for treatment of illnesses, including plant-based remedies.

Some domains of traditional knowledge may not be shared equally among community members. A traditional health practitioner, for example, may hold a wealth of knowledge relating to illnesses (be they physically, emotionally or spiritually defined), and to treatments for these illnesses. Through a process of trial and error, effective cure for, and prevention of illnesses can be identified within a community.

This knowledge can be suddenly lost if the last remaining holder of this knowledge dies without passing it on to others. Efforts to document and record domains of traditional knowledge have been undertaken with endangered language groups, while elderly speakers and holders of the knowledge remain active. Knowledge can be recorded in the form of dictionaries, such as a dictionary of place names or medical terms. Knowledge can be recorded digitally, to capture the spoken form of the knowledge, and it can be represented in books.

Without a community to practice the knowledge, the value of the knowledge can be diminished. Knowledge of the type discussed in this chapter is not artefacts or items of curiosity. This knowledge is a representation of the experiences, attitudes, beliefs, solutions, and even the code for human interaction with the physical world, with the natural world, and quite often, with the spiritual world.

The following section reports on indigenous knowledge systems to highlight the importance that these systems may hold to the groups that own and operate through them.

6.1. Humans and their environment

A well-documented dimension of traditional knowledge systems is the relationship between humans and their environment, in terms of forest conservation and animal conservation.

6.1.1. Forest conservation

Roth (2004) provides an insight into the forest conservation knowledge system of Karen-speaking village communities inhabiting tropical forests in the north of Thailand. For the Karen, the local forest is regarded as a home for animals and humans. Just as the forest supports human life, so does it sustain the life of local animals. The local Karen practice traditional forms of territorial conservation and follow their own rules governing the use of forest. They practice protection of trees, and have assigned designated forest areas for hunter-gatherer forms of collection of non-timber products.

The dependence on the forest for food forms the basis of the traditional knowledge system of the Karen people. This knowledge is passed from one generation to the next in the form of daily practice. This knowledge system represents the rules governing use of the forest, and provides a basis upon which the Karen can co-exist with the natural world.

Another well-documented group of forest dwellers practicing sustainable forest harvesting is the Penan Benalui people of Indonesian Borneo. Donovan and Puri (2004) detail the traditional knowledge of non-timber forest products of the Penan Benalui. These forest dwellers practice forms of hunter-gathering and agriculture to provide a variety of forest products for food, building materials and trade with other communities. They practice harvesting of the bark to bind animals and make storage containers, and for flooring and roofing materials in temporary forest shelters. The Penan Benalui have a specialist knowledge of resin extracted from local trees and traded. The highest quality resin, assuming a black, smooth, oily appearance, is the hardest to find, and forms the focus of much of the Penan Benalui activity. Expeditions to collect this resin involve sharing of traditional knowledge of the most promising parts of the forest for collection.

Camacho *et al.* (2012) provide insights into the forest conservation practices of the Isneg and Tingguian people of Abra Province in the northern Philippines. The practices form a system termed *lapat* which involves sustainable regulation of natural resources. The knowledge system is passed on intergenerationally. Lapat involves the use of territorial taboo in designated forest and river areas to allow the recovery of animal and plant species following a period of exploitation. In extreme cases, an entire mountain may be placed under lapat for two or more years to allow for adequate regeneration of plant species and repopulation of animal species. Once the decision is made to impose a territorial taboo, a ritual is practiced involving offerings. Enforcement of the taboo is ensured through election of community elders who assume the role of taboo enforcement workers.

A different language community is described by Burenhult and Wegener (2009) in terms of preliminary work being undertaken to record in dictionary form the sustainable forest management practices of the Orang Asli language communities inhabiting the equatorial forests of Malaysia. The Semnam, and other Aslian language communities including Jahai, Menriq, Batek, Lenoh and Maniq, have accumulated ethnobiological knowledge about the forest which forms the foundation of their sustainable forest management practices. This knowledge is transmitted intergenerationally through spoken language; these languages lack written systems. The focus of the language documentation is on preservation of local knowledge in writing. Such documentation programs with specific objectives are increasingly being looked to as a vehicle to promote language use and preservation.

Another dictionary project, outlined by Mosel (2011), is a dictionary compilation project among the approximately 500 Teop speakers of Bougainville, Papua New Guinea, focusing on development of mini-dictionaries of language specific to house building, body and health, fish, shells and trees. Through collaborative work with locals, young and old, to compile the dictionaries for use in local schools and the community, the research team of Ulrike Mosel and Ruth Spriggs sensed an increased language awareness of and pride in the mother tongue among younger speakers.

6.1.2. Animal conservation

Traditional knowledge systems can be associated with protection of animal species. Moller, Berkes, Lyver and Kislalioglu (2004) examine the traditional ecological knowledge systems of the Rakiura Māori, New Zealand's southernmost group of indigenous people, who travel by boat to 36 offshore islands known as the *Tītī Islands*, around Stewart Island, each autumn to collect the chicks of the sooty shearwater, also known by its Māori name *tītī* and more commonly as *muttonbird*. Rakiura Māori use *tītī* for food, for their feathers and down, and as a trade item. These expeditions hold both cultural and economic importance for the Rakiura Māori.

Traditional knowledge of the *tītī* is associated with traditional guidelines (*kaitiakitanga*) which form the basis of monitoring the long-term well-being of the bird populations and the quantity of chicks collected. Written records of *tītī* harvests dating back to 1927 include information of catch totals, weather conditions, and moon cycles.

6.2. Health and medicinal knowledge

Another aspect of traditional knowledge systems relates to health and medicinal knowledge, often held and administered by traditional health practitioners.

Iquito is one such community with this knowledge base. Iquito is a highly endangered language of the Zaparoan family, spoken by roughly twenty ageing people living in two villages located in the Alto

Nanay region of north-eastern Amazon. According to Jernigan (2011), Spanish records suggest that the language was once widely spoken over an extended area between the Tigre, Mazán and Amazon rivers. The Iquito moved away from the major river systems to avoid contact with missionaries and slave traders. More recent contact with rubber traders resulted in discouragement by the rubber bosses of use of Iquito and a resulting negative attitude towards the heritage language among the Iquito population. A once monolingual population became mostly bilingual in Iquito and Spanish by the 1950s, with falling rates of intergenerational transmission of Iquito.

An influx of settlers and resulting mixed marriages resulted in further decline of use of the language, while epidemics of flu, malaria and other infectious diseases took its toll on some of the older monolingual speakers. Jernigan (2011) reports that by the 1990s, Spanish had largely replaced Iquito as the preferred language of interaction among the Iquito. As a result of language documentation and revitalization efforts supported by outsiders, there has been a positive change among Iquito in their attitude towards their language.

One particular area of interest to the Iquito and linguists working with them is terminology for illnesses. Jernigan (2011) offers these examples:

- Aquíraja - involves diarrhoea and vomiting and is thought to come from being struck by a strong wind carrying bad spirits or harmful environmental influences.
- Corazonada - a dangerously strong heartbeat that comes from arguing with one's spouse
- Empacho - a digestive illness said to be caused by bad diet, involving intestinal swelling, headache, vomiting and diarrhoea
- ácusana isíicu - red, itchy spots
- musutina isíicu - white spots that are not painful
- Múcuaay itúuja - a rash caused by exposure to a rainbow, the sun or mist
- Pulsario – a worm that lives in the lower abdomen and grows bigger with emotional stress
- Saladera - persistent bad luck, especially in hunting

- Sobreparto - an illness women may suffer after giving birth that involves diarrhoea, body pain and fever
- Tabardillo - a high fever caused by bathing too quickly after working in the sun

These terms and accompanying beliefs suggest environmental, social and spiritual causes for illnesses. Within the traditional knowledge system of the Iquito are the following medical explanations documented by Jernigan (2011):

- Diarrhoea: blamed on eating greasy foods on an empty stomach
- Intestinal parasites: said to come from consuming sweet fruits like ripe plantains and caimito (Pouteria caimito)
- Blood-related illnesses and skin problems: said to come from eating fish with spotted patterns
- Babies are susceptible to mouth sores when a breastfeeding mother consumes spotted fish
- Consuming ácuta (Banisteriopsis caapi) and curarina (Potalia amara) can cleanse impurities from the body

Reporting on another language community possessing specific knowledge related to health, Adoukonou-Sagbadja, Dansi, Vodouhè and Akpagana (2006) describe the traditional cultivation of fonio millet in the Akposso and Lamba language communities of southern Togo, where fonio millet is a staple food cultivated for home consumption. Fonio is eaten with each meal of the day, and is an important food for occasions like celebrations and entertaining guests. It is also fed to domesticated animals. In addition to its dietary importance, Fonio is believed by local communities to have important medicinal properties. It is used to treat blood clots resulting from injuries or during childbirth. In addition, it is used to treat dysentery, diarrhoea, chickenpox and asthma, in addition to relief of mild stomach complaints. Fonio is also believed to be suitable for diabetics.

6.3. Terminology

One domain of language use which is often appreciated and recognized by the wider community is place names. Troy and Walsh (2008) report on terminology planning in Australia in which indigenous language revitalization efforts have focused on documentation and use of indigenous terminology. Programs include the Wemba Wemba dictionary, listing plants and animals used for food and artefact production, and local programs to identify former aboriginal names of places and reinstate these in the wider domain. Some examples of the latter include:

- Kura Yerlo (near the sea)
- Yaitya Warra Wodli (indigenous language place)

In New South Wales, there has been an increased focus in recent years on reinstating traditional aboriginal place names, and renaming of localities.

Traditional place names are also discussed by Davidson-Hunt and Berkes (2003) in relation to the Anishinaabe people in northwestern Ontario, Canada. The Anishinaabe are speakers of Algonquian which is one of the largest indigenous language groups in North America. The Anishinaabe possess traditional ecological knowledge of patterns of environmental change. This knowledge system is dynamic, involving community debate and decision-making processes for responding appropriately to environmental changes. The knowledge system is remembered through long-term communal understanding, termed *social memory*, and is passed from one generation to the next.

For the Anishinaabe, place names have evolved to link the history of the people with their occupancy of the land. The names provide an image of the physical nature of a place, its relationship with other places, and events that took place there. Examples are:

- Aagimakobawatig (a place where black ash grows beside a rapid)
- Animoshi Minis (where the howling of dogs was said to have been heard in the past)
- Gaanikooshkooshkaag Zaagaigan (a lake where a specific type of plant grows)
- Gitigaani Minis (an island where gardening occurred)
- Ogishkibwaakaaning (where wild potatoes grew)

The Anishinaabe's understanding of moon cycles and patterns is central to their knowledge system. Terms given for different stages of the moon cycle represent important events in the Anishinaabe calendar. Examples are:

- Migizi giizis (bald eagle moon)
- Miinikaa giizis (blueberrying moon)
- Manitoo giizis (Creator's moon)

In a different setting, Boden (2011) reports on the indigenous place names of the !Xoon, hunter-gatherers who inhabit Namibia. The !Xoon are speakers of Taa, which is the sole remaining language of the Tuu language family. Today there are 500 speakers of Taa in Namibia, and a further 2,000 to 4,000 speakers in Botswana. Most of the Namibian speakers of Taa are !Xoon.

Boden (2011) indicates that the majority of !Xoon place names originate from plant and animal species, often in relation to land forms or locations, and historical events. Examples are:

- Hharisi-i-!uhm (dune of the honey badgers)
- !Uhm-ma-ka-aqhnya-ka (dune that is red)
- !Ahu-sue (depression-inside)
- Hham (termite hill)
- Kunn'ai-i-!uhm (mirror dune) - a dune on the southern rim of the Aminuis salt pan on top of which the Germans had erected a heliograph for sending messages
- Xai-e (snare) - named for the great number of snares which were usually set there

The importance of terminology, and place names, to minority and indigenous groups needs to be more clearly understood. Efforts to reinstate traditional names, where they have been replaced with names from dominant languages, may provide a meaningful step towards raising the status of local languages. Such steps may be well received by the wider community, in recognition of the traditional residents of the land.

6.4. Summary

Traditional knowledge systems, as reported in this chapter, represent a sensitive and complex code for human interaction with the environment, its living and physical elements, and its resources. The code is an accumulated body of knowledge particular to a group and its natural setting. Themes of reciprocity and respect describe the relationship between humans and other entities, with care taken to preserve the environment and utilize its resources sustainably.

Dictionary projects to record plant names, medicinal knowledge, and place names are underway with some endangered language communities. Projects to reinstate place names in local areas can be significant steps for minority and indigenous groups in raising the status and appreciation of minority languages.

7. Belief systems

Traditional belief systems are typically associated with animism and the existence of a spiritual world. They relate to perceptions about the human relationship with the natural and physical worlds, and form the foundation for social rules and practice. Common themes are respect for the natural world and the importance of spiritual beliefs in the construction of personal identity (see Bird-David 1999; Harvey 2005; Willerslev 2007).

A belief system can be thought of in terms of the values of a community. A belief system can also be thought of in terms of the explanations a community has arrived at for perplexing questions such as where humans come from, what created the world and the universe, what controls the weather, plant and animal life, what controls the physical world, and what accounts for natural disasters.

Belief systems can describe the behavior, customs and ritual practices of a community at symbolic times. This could be related to agricultural cycles of planting and harvesting, human fertility, key stages in life such as initiation rites, or in response to sickness, death, or conflict. It could be associated with reinforcing kinship ties.

Belief systems, like knowledge systems, are not static. They change and evolve to reflect the needs of the community of users. Spiritual practices once deemed appropriate may one day be viewed as inappropriate and abandoned. Ritual practices once deemed central to daily life may one day lose their relevance.

Generational gaps can develop within a community whereby younger members arrive at new ideas about values, beliefs and practices. The new ideas may be conveyed through school education, media, or the Internet. Some societies may be in crisis over the divisions created by the influx of new ideas influencing younger members, and the desire of elders to adhere to traditional ways.

Communities may need the opportunity to adapt their belief systems to reflect the expectations and perceptions of the mainstream society. Some communities may require guidance from linguists, ethnographers, anthropologists and other experts in the area of language, culture and identity to enable them to overcome their internal divisions. Some communities may find themselves in conflict with other groups, particularly in the dominant society, over belief systems. There may be an important role for mediators with sensitivity to language and culture concerns to address the respective issues and help chart a path forward.

Technological developments and the access to knowledge and cultural influences provided by computers and the Internet are reaching previously isolated communities. This form of digitalized contact with the outside world will bring new challenges and new opportunities to indigenous cultures. Some communities may embrace the technology and utilize it to strengthen their language, and improve the attitudes towards the language and beliefs among their younger speakers. Other communities may see younger members shift away from the heritage language and beliefs in increasing numbers. We are, needless to say, facing uncertain times for the world's remaining endangered languages.

MacDonald (2011) highlights three broad characteristics of indigenous belief systems. First, indigenous communities are concerned with the land. Relationship with the land provides a sense of identity, and ritual activity relating to the land is concerned with sustainability and renewal. Second, indigenous communities are concerned with their relationships with each other, with a focus on the community rather than the individual. This relationship can extend to animals and plants. Third, indigenous communities are concerned with fertility in a broad sense, relating to the fertility of humans, animals and plants. Rituals are associated with enhancing and restoring life, around times of planting and harvesting, and in times of sickness.

This chapter reports on various indigenous belief systems in an attempt to capture the significance of these systems to the language communities who own them.

7.1. Relationship with the land

Attachment to the land is central to indigenous beliefs. Brown and Cousins (2001) report on Native American relationships with the land. The view held is that nobody owns the land, but it is the responsibility of inhabitants to watch over and care for the land. In return, the land cares for its inhabitants. This reciprocity is at the heart of native American beliefs and the sacred. They view the land as containing spiritual powers, and thus look to the land for spiritual guidance and support. This belief system shapes moral judgment and behavior.

In a different ethnographic study, Long, Tecle and Burnette (2003) describe the belief systems of the White Mountain Apache Tribe of Arizona. The physical, mental and spiritual worlds of the White Mountain Apache interact to the extent that people's behavior is believed to affect the conditions of places. Wetland areas hold special significance for the White Mountain Apache, and many local terms relate to the health of waterways. The loss of a natural spring, representing an important source of fresh water, may be the result of social collapse within the White Mountain Apache community. A local term, *Gozhoo*, describes the return of social harmony and a positive relationship between humans and the environment, represented by a return to good human health and the return of a healthy wetland area.

Lewis and Sheppard (2005) report that the Cheam people of British Columbia also hold spiritual beliefs centered around traditional notions of respect for the land. For the Cheam, speakers of the Halkomelem language, the land was created to provide equally for all living things, including humans, animals, and plants. Central to the Cheam value system is a strong sense and expression of consideration for the needs of other living things when resources are taken from the environment. In practice, this sense of respect ensures that the Cheam leave sufficient resources in the environment to ensure the continuing survival of other living communities. For the Cheam, the mountains, water, trees, plants and animals are sacred. The result of these beliefs is the sustainable use of the environment.

The Cheam seek and gain spiritual renewal from contact with the environment. The Cheam believe that sadness or troublesome feelings can be alleviated by walking through the forest and letting branches brush against the skin. This brushing action is said to take away the bad feelings. The land also strengthens people's connection with their ancestors. This is the case for the Cheam when they bathe in a part of a river which their ancestors had used for bathing.

7.2. Spiritual beliefs

Animist and spiritual belief systems have been extensively documented among indigenous groups. Roth (2004), for example, provides an insight into the belief system of one group, the Karen-speaking village communities inhabiting tropical forests in the north of Thailand. These communities have strong beliefs in spirits. For the Karen, the local forest is regarded as a home for the spirits. These include the spirits of the forest, water and wind, as well as ancestral spirits. The local Karen have assigned designated spiritual forest areas such as burial forests, homes to ancestral spirits, and other parts of the forest near rivers and on mountaintops for movement of forest, water and wind spirits.

Another documented spiritual belief system in Southeast Asia are the beliefs and practices of the Bisu people of Northern Thailand. The daily activities of the Bisu of Thailand revolve around the spiritual world. Gustafson (2010) provides considerable detail about these beliefs and practices. The Bisu believe that the spiritual world exerts control over their lives. Some of the documented spirits are:

- Ang Cao: village spirit
- Yum Dae: house spirit
- Song Khong Dae: forest spirit
- Pum Dae: grave spirit

For the Bisu, accidents, illness, natural disaster and other forms of misfortune are attributed to discontented spirits.

Another well-documented group holding animist beliefs is the Penan Benalui people of Indonesian Borneo. Donovan and Puri (2004) provide insights into the belief systems of these forest dwellers. For the Penan Benalui, the forest is home to the spirits which are believed to deceive the Penan Benalui during their hunter-gatherer expeditions. Precautions are taken before and during hunter-gatherer expeditions to bring good luck and conceal their plans from the spirits. The Penan Benalui have a specialist knowledge of resin extracted from local trees and traded with the outside world. Expeditions to collect this resin involve wearing black clothing as a symbol of good luck and not talking openly about their expedition plans for fear of alerting the spirits.

Spiritual beliefs are also documented in Ghana. The rain forests of Ghana, once abundant, became depleted after the area was opened up for commercial logging. Following the loggers were settlers who practiced shifting cultivation, depleting the soils of nutrients and effectively preventing regrowth of secondary forest. The result, Appiah-Opoku (2007) reports, was that by 1991, only 2.1 million of Ghana's original 8.1 million hectares of rainforest remained.

There are remaining isolated pockets of rainforest canopy in Ghana, in sacred groves, which were not subject to deforestation. Appiah-Opoku (2007) explains that between 2,000 and 3,200 groves are traditionally protected tracts of ancestral land. They are regarded by the local people as ancestral dwelling places, and include forests, rivers and lakes that have remained undisturbed.

The sacred groves are protected through local taboos, and belief that failure to respect the taboos could result in bad luck, sickness and even death. Today, these sacred groves serve as protected refuges for animal and plant species, and provide important watershed areas.

7.3. Traditional health beliefs

To mirror the discussion on health and medicine in the previous chapter, this section explores the same domain of language use from the perspective of beliefs. Maskarinec *et al.* (2011) describe the traditional health beliefs and practices of the Wa'ap people inhabiting the Yap islands in Western Micronesia. The population of 11,200 spread across four islands are speakers of Yapese, Ulithian, Woleaian and Satawalese. The Wa'ap place high value on kinship relationships and provision of care at times of sickness of a community member. The Wa'ap have not responded favourably to modern Western medicine and Western-trained medical practitioners, instead, showing a preference for local medicine prescribed and administered by local medicine practitioners. These practitioners have a strong relationship with the patient and their families, and this relationship is highly valued.

The Yap follow traditional practices associated with hygiene and feeding, and value the central role for the family in the provision of care. Death within a family initiates a complex series of rituals and exchange focusing on reaffirming kinship ties within the community. These rituals reestablish a sense of personal identity within the community. These practices and rituals have come under threat through contact with external religious and cultural influences.

Dove (2010) arrives at similar findings in Ghanaian communities, in terms of resistance to efforts at implementing Western medical practices. The process has importance in terms of beliefs and ethics for medical care in parts of Ghana where traditional medical practitioners are still widely respected and utilized by an estimated 80% of the population. Traditional use of herbal remedies is linked to spiritual beliefs and the exercise of taboos in times of sickness and pregnancy. There is belief among indigenous groups in Ghana that the following foods should be avoided during pregnancy:

- Honey: causes respiratory problems for the child at birth
- Bambara beans: causes respiratory and skin problems for the child at birth
- Corn flour: linked to heavy bleeding during delivery
- Shea butter: can cause difficulty during delivery
- Eggs, fresh meat, fresh milk, cold and sugary foods: make the unborn baby large, contributing to a difficult delivery and possible death of the mother

In addition, there is belief that the following places are to be avoided during pregnancy:

- Market places: have too much noise for the baby and are vulnerable to negative spirits
- Funerals: have powerful spiritual activities and are vulnerable to negative forces
- Shrines: have powerful spiritual movements and are vulnerable to negative forces
- Forests and bush: are vulnerable to negative spirits
- Rivers: are vulnerable to negative spirits
- The father's family house: is vulnerable to negative spirits

Traditional remedies which the locals have strong beliefs in, include:

- Kagiligu-tim (charcoal): used on pregnant women to facilitate easy delivery
- Incense: burned for a child to inhale the smoke causing sneezing and regaining of consciousness
- Nanwa (a type of salt added to reduce acidity of foods): mixed with shea butter for treating upset stomachs and applied to boils
- Charcoal and herbs: ground and applied to the child's body to treat fever

Dove (2010) comments that traditional medicinal beliefs are creative and dynamic, with some holding potential to be applied more generally in public medicine to treat illnesses.

Similarly, in an African setting, Patel (2011) reports on the provision of public health in parts of the continent where traditional health healers continue to perform an important role in the treatment of mental health. Patel raises the question of whether traditional taxonomies of mental health could be mapped onto Western descriptions to provide a stronger evidential basis for applying treatments in a range of cultural settings. Patel recognizes the scope for improved local practice in medical care by recognizing and working with the traditional approaches to health care, reiterating the World Health Organization's declaration that traditional medicine, when used properly, can make an important contribution to public health.

7.4. Summary

Belief systems based on worldviews, the relationship to land, the role of spiritual entities, and the use of taboos, have shaped the daily lives and rituals of the indigenous communities reported in this chapter. The book began with reference to an enclave community in the north of Thailand, and the comment by village elders of the importance of spiritual beliefs to their way of life. This spiritual importance can be interpreted as a key to the continued identity of the language users.

8. Preserving cultural identity

The preceding chapters of this book have highlighted the role of language, knowledge systems and belief systems for indigenous groups in various geographical settings in the world. This chapter considers the significance of these three dimensions of cultural expression on individual and collective identity.

8.1. Cultural identity

Construction of cultural identity has been examined in an African setting. Tchindjang, Bodpa and Ngamgne (2008) view language in terms of its role in the construction of cultural identities. They see language as a means for people to collectively express their heritage, their soul, and their spirit. Language symbolizes collective thought and collective expression, passed from one generation to the next. It is a source of knowledge, a source of beliefs, and a source of identity. In this context, language loss threatens the survival of cultural identities and cultural diversity. Language is also broadly linked to self-determination and rural development. There is a call for educational reform which enables students to construct their social identities, master their mother tongue, and discover their history and the accomplishments of their ancestors. Literacy programs should be designed around practical learning which can benefit people, providing a means to learn about first aid, sanitation and soil enrichment. Literacy can be a means to develop expertise in managing water, soil and food supplies.

Benton (2007) reflects on the nature of Māori identity, suggesting that it is strongly associated with *Whanaungatanga* (sense of relationship through shared ancestry). There is a strong identification of Māori with tribal affiliation and connection with traditionally owned lands. Māori refer to themselves as *tangata whenua* (people of the land). Thus, Māori language revitalization, while critically important to Māori, may for some Māori be secondary to land rights in terms of safeguarding the identity of their people.

In a different setting, Arka (2010) has documented the Rongga language, part of the Austronesian language group, and spoken by an estimated 5,000 speakers in three villages in Flores, Indonesia. Most villagers are conversant in Rongga, Bahasa Indonesia, and Manggarai, a more dominant regional language. The local schools teach Manggarai and Bahasa Indonesia. Rongga is not taught in local schools. Bahasa Indonesia is widely used in the area, in contact with doctors, lawyers, teachers and merchants, and in the Catholic Church, to which most locals belong. Bahasa Indonesia is seen as a status language.

Arka (2010) reports on the efforts among the Rongga people to maintain their cultural identity in the face of external cultural influences which have arisen through Catholic missionary contact, schooling, development and modernization. Recent efforts among the Rongga people have been directed at preserving their cultural identity. They have focused their attention on a ritual dance termed *Vera*, which is performed on special occasions such as the start of the planting season. The dance with accompanying song is performed by two lines of adults, one male and one female, starting at midnight and lasting till dawn. The verse contains ritual language particular to the Rongga people. The dance is seen as a vehicle for perpetuating cultural identity among the Rongga, containing within the verse traditional knowledge, and providing a spiritual and cultural link between the Rongga and their ancestors.

Recent threats to the preservation of the ritual dance of the Rongga are numerous, and are reflected in skill in performing the dance not being satisfactorily passed onto younger generations. These threats stem from the erosion of the traditional belief system underpinning the dance through the introduction of Catholicism and modern education; competition for attention from radio, television and movies and the appeal of Western culture (song and dance) and sports; a perceived boring element attached to the long, repetitive patterns of the dance; and the loss of ritual language knowledge required to perform the dance.

Steps are underway to document the ritual dance and to preserve it as a record in audio and visual formats for future generations. A Rongga Language Documentation Project was recently established to promote teaching and performance of the ritual dance; the continuity of the project is uncertain.

8.2. Indigenous education

One domain in which identity can be strengthened is education. According to Cherubini, Kitchen and Trudeau (2009), the First Nations peoples of Canada have long advocated for education to take account of indigenous linguistic and cultural traditions. The Native Teacher Education Programs in Canada seek to recruit indigenous people into teaching, with a hope that they will be central in the delivery of bilingual programs which cater to the needs of indigenous children and their communities. Within the program is scope for indigenous teachers to adopt local paradigms of teaching and learning.

A consequence of such programs is the identification of teachers as indigenous, and identification of their teaching practice as informed by indigenous paradigms.

The Navajo Nation Council, a First Nations group of North America, regards "the human resources of the Navajo Nation as its most valuable resource" (Navajo Nation Council 2000: ii), and stipulates its expectation that all Navajo people will experience an education which provides competence in Navajo language skills and knowledge of Navajo culture, in addition to competence in English language skills and knowledge of American culture. This goal fits inside the value system of the Navajo people to preserve and perpetuate their native language, culture and identity. The philosophy of the Navajo Nation has a spiritual dimension, reflecting the Navajo view that they are "one with nature and the universe" (2000: v), and their ancestors go back to the beginning of time.

8.3. Summary

We are faced with a collective responsibility to promote among the world's peoples positive senses of identity. This identity can be personal; it can be collective. We are also faced with a collective responsibility to show respect towards the linguistic and cultural heritage of others.

The future for the world's minority languages rests in the strength of their numbers of speakers, and the success in transmitting language, knowledge, beliefs and a positive sense of identity to successive generations. The conditions for language maintenance are shaped by the messages coming from global bodies such as the United Nations and its relevant agencies, the language policies of nation states, the willingness of schools to respond to opportunities and needs in the area of heritage language instruction, the commitment of indigenous teachers to promote positive senses of pride and identity towards heritage languages among minority groups, and the support provided by linguists and research centers.

All of these dimensions shape language policy, shape attitudes to language, and shape identity. The stronger the sense of identity, the more efforts are likely to be directed towards maintaining language in the face of challenges brought on through contact with broader society.

9. Conclusion

Humans have populated most parts of the world, establishing communities with distinctive cultures and practices. Some communities are nomadic. Some are hunter-gatherers. Some have developed complex systems of interaction with their environment based on sustainable use of resources. Some communities have over-exploited the natural environment, changing it markedly.

The common feature of human settlement of the land is the development and use of complex language systems. These languages serve multiple purposes for their speakers. They enable communication among members of a community. This is important for security, for hunting and food collection, and for social cohesion. Languages capture the knowledge and experiences people have, based on their interaction with the environment. This knowledge can include methods of hunting, food collection and resource use. It can include descriptions of the physical landscape, plants and animals. It can include climatic and weather patterns, and tidal, seasonal and celestial changes. The knowledge can include descriptions of illnesses and medical use of plants and minerals.

Humans have developed cultural practices which are conveyed and expressed through dance, song, drama, storytelling and oral histories. Some communities have developed writing systems to complement the spoken language. In this way, literacy, the ability to read and write, developed.

Humans also developed complex belief systems, representing their self and worldview, their understanding of how humans were created or evolved, their social values, their taboos, and their code for human interaction with the physical, living and spiritual worlds. Many communities recognize spiritual entities, including ancestral spirits, and spirits associated with water, other attributes of the physical environment, and attributes of the living world. Rituals and practice have evolved to reflect beliefs about the role of spirits in daily life.

Today, there are over 7,000 documented languages, including sign languages. This number indicates great linguistic and cultural diversity that defines humankind. Through oral and, in some cases, written means, communities have passed on their language from one generation to the next. Over time, languages can change to reflect the needs of their community of speakers. These changes in the language are transmitted intergenerationally to ensure continuity of the language and culture, and continuity of the shared knowledge and shared values. The accumulated knowledge of a community of speakers, and the belief systems they created, are captured and expressed in the language.

When a language dies, the loss is more than a collection of words tied together in a grammatical system. When a language dies, it takes with it the culture of its speakers, the accumulated knowledge its speakers have about their environment and surroundings, including place names and the beliefs of the community. Collectively, the language, culture, knowledge and beliefs define the identity of the community of speakers.

Of the 7,000 or more documented languages, a growing number are becoming endangered as the clock ticks. This is due to a range of factors. Languages can become endangered when their speakers come into contact with another language used by a more dominant, powerful or developed society. There may be subsequent language shift, particularly among younger speakers, away from the mother tongue and towards the new language. This shift may be voluntary; it may be forced or coerced. The shift may be resisted by a community, or it may be embraced.

Languages can become endangered when the community of speakers become endangered through sickness, conflict or subjugation. When a community of speakers lose their homes, their right to reside on traditional land, or even their right to live, languages can die out.

Languages can become endangered when the language loses its traditional domains or is not used in new domains. Language endangerment can be associated with declining use of the language in the home, in social settings, in commercial interactions, and in rituals.

A key factor in language survival is the role of education. While a community of speakers has full control over the transmission of language and knowledge to future generations, the language can be safe. However, schools set up and administered by outsiders can be a catalyst for language loss if the local children are taught in a new language. In the past, education has greatly enhanced the status and number of speakers of a relatively small number of dominant languages, and has seen the weakening and demise of a comparatively large number of minority languages.

Today there is growing appreciation of the important role school-based education can play in language maintenance and language revitalization. Through bilingual, multilingual, immersion and mother tongue-based forms of education, children can be exposed in schools to heritage languages and languages used in the wider community, with a positive effect overall on cognitive development and engagement with learning for children from minority language backgrounds.

At the international, regional, state and local levels, language policy can impact either negatively or positively on attitudes towards linguistic and cultural diversity. The rights of minority and indigenous communities to use and teach their language are now being safeguarded by an increasing number of states, in some cases, through official recognition of the value and significance of minority and indigenous languages.

Governments are involved in discussions and debate at regional and international levels about how to respond to the linguistic and cultural diversity found within their territorial borders, while serving nationalist goals of preserving unity and ensuring domestic commonality of efforts to serve national interests.

Some countries have legislated towards a more diverse linguistic representation of its people, officially recognizing more than one language. In some cases, attempts have been made to embrace a wide range of nationalities and linguistic groups.

In an effort to reverse previous patterns of language loss over time, including the loss of some indigenous sign languages, and to safeguard the knowledge and beliefs held within the language, linguists have often led the way in programs of language documentation, language attitude surveys, and language revitalization, working closely with specific communities of speakers.

Efforts are underway to improve local people's attitudes towards their heritage language with a growing number of endangered languages to improve the conditions for language revival and increase the range of domains in which the language is used, focusing particularly on language use in the home, the school and the local community.

Language revitalization efforts have involved development of written scripts for languages lacking an orthography, development of dictionaries and books for use in local schools and community education resource centers, training of local speakers of the language to become teachers in local schools, and development of appropriate models of bilingual or multilingual education to accommodate the dual needs of preserving the heritage language and providing good opportunities for all children to participate fully in educational and vocational activities in the wider community.

In a broader sense, language revitalization can be considered as part of a process of development, often in a rural setting, in which care is taken to allow communities of speakers to adapt to a changing economic and technological environment and changing opportunities, without losing their heritage language, their culture and their values. In this way, self-pride in the heritage language and culture can be preserved, as can self-identification with the language and culture.

How many of the world's languages will survive for future generations to use and identify with? The answer depends partly on the collective efforts of countries and regional groupings to promote positive attitudes and policies towards preserving linguistic and cultural diversity. The answer also depends partly on the attitudes of individuals and communities of speakers towards their own heritage language.

Linguists, ethnographers, and academics working in related areas of language, culture and identity have a responsibility and an opportunity to lead the way in promoting positive attitudes and actions at the state level. Language policy is more than government legislation and policy documents. It is about goals, attitudes and efforts of language speakers, and the local community and schools, to ensure vitality of the language and to ensure that future generations benefit from the cultural richness that is embedded in the language.

Nettle and Romaine (2000) make the case that the right to practice their own language and culture is inalienable. This right includes self-determination over use of the environment, based on the realization that indigenous communities have a long-term interest in sustainable practice. When denied the right to access the environment, their knowledge, practices and language can die out. Economically, they can suffer. For Nettle and Romaine (2000), the first causes of language loss are not linguistic, but rather stresses on the society and its traditional practices.

There is scope to reintroduce languages that have lost their last remaining elderly native speakers, provided that there remains a community of people who share a vision to re-establish a linguistic link with their past. This is starting to happen with isolated languages. The challenge is to recapture the knowledge and beliefs that were once expressed through the language, and once helped to define the identity of autonomous groups of people.

References

Adegjiba, Efurosibina 2004. Language Policy and Planning in Nigeria. *Current Issues in Language Planning*. 5/3, 181-246.
Adoukonou-Sagbadja, Hubert / Dansi, Alexandre / Vodouhè, Raymond / Akpagana, K. 2006. Indigenous Knowledge and Traditional Conservation of Fonio Millet (Digitaria exilis, Digitaria iburua) in Togo. *Biodiversity and Conservation* 15, 2379-2395.
Ansaldo, Umberto. 2010. Identity Alignment and Language Creation in Multilingual Communities. *Language Sciences* 32/6, 615-623.
Appiah-Opoku, Seth 2007. Indigenous Beliefs and Environmental Stewardship: A Rural Ghana Experience. *Journal of Cultural Geography* 24/21, 79-98.
Arka, I Wayan 2010. Maintaining *Vera* in Rongga: Struggles over Culture, Tradition, and Language in Modern Manggarai, Flores, Indonesia. In Florey, Margaret (ed.) *Endangered Languages of Austronesia*. Oxford: Oxford University Press, 90-109.
Arviso, Marie / Holm, Wayne 2001. Tse'hootsooı́ di O'lta'gi Dine' Bizaad Bihoo' aah: A Navajo Immersion Program at Fort Defiance, Arizona. In Hinton, Leanne / Hale, Ken (eds) *The Green Book of Language Revitalization in Practice*. San Diego: Academic Press, 203-216.
Austin, Peter 2003. Australia. In Comrie, Bernard / Matthews, Stephen / Polinsky, Maria (eds) *Atlas of Languages: The Origins and Development of Languages Throughout the World*. Sydney: ABC Books, 108-123.
Baker, Colin 2011. *Foundations of Bilingual Education and Bilingualism*. Clevedon, UK: Multilingual Matters.
Barrena, Andoni / Idiazabal, Itziar / Juaristi, Patxi / Junyent, Carme / Ortega, Paul / Uranga, Belen 2006. World Languages Review: Some Data. In Cunningham, Denis / Ingram, David / Sumbuk,

Kenneth (eds) *Language Diversity in the Pacific: Endangerment and Survival.* Clevedon: Multilingual Matters, 15-23.

Bauer, Kira Russo 2007. Protecting Indigenous Spiritual Values. *Peace Review: A Journal of Social Justice* 19/3, 343-349.

Beier, Christine / Lev, Michael 2006. The Iquito Language Documentation Project: Developing Team-based Methods for Language Documentation. *Linguistic Discovery* 4/1.

Benet-Martínez, Verónica / Haritatos, Jana 2005. Bicultural Identity Integration (BII): Components and Psychosocial Antecedents. *Journal of Personality* 73/4, 1015-1050.

Benton, Nena 1989. Education, Language Decline and Language Revitalisation: The Case of Maori in New Zealand. *Language and Education* 3/2, 65-82.

Benton, Richard 2007. Mauri or Mirage? The Status of the Maori Language in Aotearoa New Zealand in the Third Millennium. In Tsui, Amy / Tollefson, James (eds) *Language Policy, Culture, and Identity in Asian Contexts.* Mahwah, NJ: Lawrence Erlbaum, 163-181.

Berkes, Fikret 1993. Traditional Ecological Knowledge in Perspective. In Inglis, Julian (ed.) *Traditional Ecological Knowledge: Concepts and Cases.* Ottawa: International Program on Traditional Ecological Knowledge and International Development Research Centre, 1-9.

Berkes, Fikret / Colding, Johan / Folke, Carl 2000. Rediscovery of Traditional Ecological Knowledge as Adaptive Management. *Ecological Applications* 10/5, 1251-1262.

Berry, John 1990. Psychology of Acculturation. In Goldberger, Nancy / Veroff, Jody (eds) *The Culture and Psychology Reader.* New York: New York University Press, 457-488.

Bialystok, Ellen 2005. *Consequences of Bilingualism for Cognitive Development.* New York: Oxford University Press.

Bird-David, Nurit 1999. "Animism" Revisited: Personhood, Environment, and Relational Epistemology. *Current Anthropology* 40/S1, S67-S91.

Boden, Gertrud 2011. The Documentation of Place Names in an Endangered Language Environment: A Case Study of the!Xoon in Southern Omaheke, Namibia. *Anthropological Linguistics* 53/1, 34-76.

Bouju, Jacky 2003. Nommo: The Spirit of Water: In the Dogon World. *Leonardo* 36/4, 279-280.

Bradley, David 2005. Language Policy and Language Endangerment in China. *International Journal of the Sociology of Language* 173: 1-21.

Bradley, David 2006. Endangered Languages of China and South-East Asia. In Cunningham, Denis / Ingram, David / Sumbuk, Kenneth (eds) *Language Diversity in the Pacific: Endangerment and Survival.* Clevedon: Multilingual Matters, 112-120.

Bradley, David / Bradley, Maya 2002. Language Policy and Language Maintenance: Yi in China. In Bradley, David / Bradley, Maya (eds) *Language Endangerment and Language Maintenance.* London: RoutledgeCurzon, 77-97.

Brosius, Peter 1997. Endangered Forest, Endangered People: Environmentalist Representations of Indigenous Knowledge. *Human Ecology* 25/1, 47-69.

Brown, Joseph Epes / Cousins, Emily 2001. *Teaching Spirits: Understanding Native American Religious Traditions.* Oxford: Oxford University Press.

Burenhult, Niclaus / Wegener, Claudia 2009. Preliminary Notes on Phonology, Orthography and Vocabulary of Semnam (Austroasiatic, Malay Peninsula). *Journal of the Southeast Asian Linguistics Society* 1, 283-312.

Camacho, Leni / Combalicer, Marilyn / Yeo-Chang, Youn / Combalicer, Edwin / Carandang, Antonio / Camacho, Sofronio / de Luna, Catherine / Rebugio, Lucrecio 2012. Traditional Forest Conservation Knowledge/Technologies in the Cordillera, Northern Philippines. *Forest Policy and Economics* 22, 3-8.

Campbell, Lyle 2012. Classification of the Indigenous Languages of South America. In Campbell, Lyle / Grondona, Veronica (eds) *The Indigenous Languages of South America: A Comprehensive Guide.* Berlin: De Gruyter Mouton, 59-166.

Cenoz, Jasone / Gorter, Durk 2008. Applied Linguistics and the Use of Minority Languages in Education. In Cenoz, Jasone / Gorter,

Durk (eds) *Multilingualism and Minority Languages*. Amsterdam: John Benjamins, 5-12.

Cherubini, Lorenzo / Kitchen, Julian / Trudeau, Lyn 2009. Having the Spirit Within to Vision: New Aboriginal Teachers' Commitment to Reclaiming Space. *Canadian Journal of Native Education* 32/9, 38-51.

Coluzzi, Paolo 2010. Endangered Languages in Borneo: A Survey among the Iban and Murut (Lun Bawang) in Temburong, Brunei. *Oceanic Linguistics* 49/1, 119-143.

Council of Europe 1992. *European Charter for Regional or Minority Languages*. Strasbourg: Council of Europe.

Crawford, James 2000. *At War With Diversity: US Language Policy in an Age of Anxiety*. Clevedon: Multilingual Matters.

Crevels, Mily 2012. Language Endangerment in South America: The Clock is Ticking. In Campbell, Lyle / Grondona, Verónica (eds) *The Indigenous Languages of South America: A Comprehensive Guide*. Berlin: De Gruyter Mouton, 167-233.

Crowley, Terry 1999. Linguistic Diversity in the Pacific: A Review Article. *Journal of Sociolinguistics* 3/1, 81-103.

Crystal, David 2010. *The Cambridge Encyclopedia of Language (Third Edition)*. Cambridge: Cambridge University Press.

Davidson-Hunt, Iain / Berkes, Fikret 2003. Learning as You Journey: Anishinaabe Perception of Social-ecological Environments and Adaptive Learning. *Conservation Ecology* 8/1, 5.

Davis, Jeffrey 2010. *Hand Talk: Sign Language Among American Indian Nations*. Cambridge: Cambridge University Press.

de Swaan, Abram 2004. Endangered Languages, Sociolinguistics, and Linguistic Sentimentalism. *European Review* 12/4, 567-580.

Donovan, Deanna / Puri, Rajindra 2004. Learning from Traditional Knowledge of Non-timber Forest Products: Penan Benalui and the Autecology of *Aquilaria* in Indonesian Borneo. *Ecology and Society* 9/3, 3.

Dove, Nah 2010. A Return to Traditional Health Care Practices: A Ghanaian Study. *Journal of Black Studies* 40/5, 823-834.

Ellis, Stephen 2005. Meaningful Consideration? A Review of Traditional Knowledge in Environmental Decision Making. *Arctic* 58/1, 66-77.

England, Nora 2007. The Influence of Mayan-speaking Linguists on the State of Mayan Linguistics. In Austin, Peter / Simpson, Andrew (eds) *Endangered Languages*. Hamburg: Helmut Buske Verlag, 93-111.

Errington, Joseph 2008. *Linguistics in a Colonial World: A Story of Language, Meaning, and Power*. Malden, MA: Blackwell.

Evans, Nicholas 2007. Warramurrungunji Undone: Australian Languages in the 51st Millennium. In Austin, Peter / Simpson, Andrew (eds) *Endangered Languages*. Hamburg: Helmut Buske Verlag, 19-44.

Fishman, Joshua 1991. *Reversing Language Shift. Theoretical and Empirical Foundations of Assistance to Threatened Languages*. Clevedon, UK: Multilingual Matters.

Gadgil, Madhav / Berkes, Fikret / Folke, Carl 1993. Indigenous Knowledge for Biodiversity Conservation. *Ambio* 22, 151-156.

Grenoble, Lenore 2003. *Language Policy in the Soviet Union*. Dordrecht: Kluwer Academic Publishers.

Grenoble, Lenore / Whaley, Lindsay 2006. *Saving Languages: An Introduction to Language Revitalization*. Cambridge: Cambridge University Press.

Griffiths, Sascha Sebastian / Robson, Laura 2010. Cultural Ecologies of Endangered Languages: The Cases of Wawa and Njanga. *Anthropological Linguistics* 52/2, 217-238.

Gustafson, Kari Ann 2010. *Testing a Method for Evaluating Key Translation Terms Using Bisu*. MA thesis, Payap University, Thailand.

Hajek, John 2006. On the Edge of the Pacific: Indonesia and East Timor. In Cunningham, Denis / Ingram, David / Sumbuk, Kenneth (eds) *Language Diversity in the Pacific: Endangerment and Survival*. Clevedon: Multilingual Matters, 121-130.

Hale, Ken 1992. On Endangered Languages and the Safeguarding of Diversity. *Language* 68/1, 1-3.

Harvey, Graham 2005. *Animism: Respecting the Living World*. New York: Columbia University Press.

Hinton, Leanne 2001. The Master-Apprentice Language Learning Program. In Hinton, Leanne / Hale, Ken (eds) *The Green Book of Language Revitalization in Practice.* San Diego: Academic Press, 217-226.

Jernigan, Kevin 2011. Dietary Restrictions in Healing among Speakers of Iquito, an Endangered Language of the Peruvian Amazon. *Journal of Ethnobiology and Ethnomedicine* 7/20, 1-20.

Joseph, John 2004. *Language and Identity: National, Ethnic, Religious.* Basingstoke: Palgrave Macmillan.

Kasanga, Luanga 2010. Streetwise English and French Advertising in Multilingual DR Congo: Symbolism, Modernity, and Cosmopolitan Identity. *International Journal of the Sociology of Language* 206, 181-205.

King, Jeanette 2001. Te Kohanga Reo: Maori Language Revitalization. In Hinton, Leanne / Hale, Ken (eds) *The Green Book of Language Revitalization in Practice.* San Diego: Academic Press, 119-128.

King, Kendall 2001. *Language Revitalization Process and Prospects: Quichua in the Ecuadorian Andes.* Clevedon, UK: Multilingual Matters.

Kouega, Jean-Paul 2007. The Language Situation in Cameroon. *Current Issues in Language Planning* 8/1, 3-93.

Krauss, Michael 1992a. Statement of Michael Krauss, representing the Linguistic Society of America. In Senate, U.S. *Native American Languages Act of 1991: Hearing before the Select Committee on Indian Affairs.* Washington, DC: U.S. Government Printing Office, 18-22.

Krauss, Michael 1992b. The World's Languages in Crisis. *Language* 68/1, 4-10.

Krauss, Michael 1997. The Indigenous Languages of the North: A Report on their Present State. Northern Minority Languages: Problems of Survival. *Senri Ethnological Studies* 44, 1-34.

Krauss, Michael 2007. Native Languages of Alaska. In Miyaoka, Osahito / Sakiyama, Osamu / Krauss, Michael (eds) *The Vanishing Languages of the Pacific Rim.* Oxford: Oxford University Press, 406-417.

Ladefoged, Peter 1992. Another View of Endangered Languages. *Language* 68, 809-811.

Legere, Karsten 2006. Language Endangerment in Tanzania: Identifying and Maintaining Endangered Languages. *South African Journal of African Languages* 3, 99-112.

Lewis, John / Sheppard, Stephen 2005. Ancient Values, New Challenges: Indigenous Spiritual Perceptions of Landscapes and Forest Management. *Society & Natural Resources: An International Journal* 18/10, 907-920.

Lewis, Paul / Simons, Gary 2010. *Assessing Endangerment: Expanding Fisherman's GIDS.* <www.lingv.ro/resources/scm_images/RRL-02-2010-Lewis.pdf>

Lewis, Paul / Simons, Gary / Fennig, Charles (eds) 2013. *Ethnologue: Languages of the World, Seventeenth edition.* Dallas, TX: SIL International. <www.ethnologue.com>

Lodhi, Abdulaziz 1993. The Language Situation in Africa Today. *Nordic Journal of African Studies* 2/1, 79-86.

Long, Jonathan / Tecle, Aregai / Burnette, Benrita 2003. Cultural Foundations for Ecological Restoration on the White Mountain Apache Reservation. *Conservation Ecology* 8/1, 4.

MacDonald, Mary 2011. The Primitive, the Primal, and the Indigenous in the Study of Religion. *Journal of the American Academy of Religion* 79/4, 814-826.

Maffi, Luisa 2002. Endangered Languages, Endangered Knowledge. *International Social Science Journal* 173/3, 385-393.

Marcos, Sylvia (ed.) 2010. *Women and Indigenous Religions.* Santa. Barbara, CA: Praeger.

Maskarinec, Gregory / Yalmadau, Fr Kelly / Maluchmai, Maryann / Tun, Petra / Yinnifel, Cyril / Hancock, Thane 2011. Palliative Care and Traditional Practices of Death and Dying in Wa'ab (Yap Proper) and in the Outer Islands of Yap. *Hawai'i Medical Journal* 70/11, 27-30.

Massini-Cagliari, Gladis 2003. Language Policy in Brazil: Monolingualism and Linguistic Prejudice. *Language Policy* 3, 3-23.

Matthews, Stephen / Polisky, Maria 2003. Europe and Eurasia. In Comrie, Bernard / Matthews, Stephen / Polinsky, Maria (eds) *Atlas of Languages: The Origins and Development of Languages Throughout the World.* Sydney: ABC Books, 36-55.

McConvell, Patrick / Thieberger, Nicholas 2006. Keeping Track of Indigenous Language Endangerment in Australia. In Cunningham, Denis / Ingram, David / Sumbuk, Kenneth (eds) *Language Diversity in the Pacific: Endangerment and Survival.* Clevedon: Multilingual Matters, 54-84.

Meek, Barbra 2010. *We Are Our Language: An Ethnography of Language Revitalization in a Northern Athabaskan Community.* Tucson, AZ: University of Arizona Press.

Moller, Henrik / Berkes, Fikret / Lyver, Philip O'Brian / Kislalioglu, Mina 2004. Combining Science and Traditional Ecological Knowledge: Monitoring Populations for Co-management. *Ecology and Society* 9/3, 2.

Morgan, Gerald 2001. Welsh: A European Case of Language Maintenance. In Hinton, Leanne / Hale, Ken (eds) *The Green Book of Language Revitalization in Practice.* San Diego: Academic Press, 107-113.

Mosel, Ulrike 2011. Lexicography in Endangered Language Communities. In Austin, Peter / Sallabank, Julia (eds) *Language Documentation and Description.* Cambridge: Cambridge University Press, 337-353.

Moseley, Christopher (ed.) 2010. *Atlas of the World's Languages in Danger (3rd Edition).* Paris: UNESCO Publishing. <www.unesco.org/culture/en/endangeredlanguages/atlas>

National Indigenous Languages Policy of Australia 2009. <arts.gov.au/indigenous/languages>

Navaho Nation Council 2000. *T'aa Sha Bik'ehgo Dine Bi Na Nitin Doo Ihoo'aah (Diné Cultural Content Standards for Students).* Office of Dine Culture, Language & Community Service, Division of Dine Education.

Nettle, Daniel / Romaine, Suzanne 2000. *Vanishing Voices: The Extinction of the World's Languages.* Oxford: Oxford University Press.

New Zealand Human Rights Commission Languages in Aotearoa New Zealand Te Waka a Reo - Statement on Language Policy 2009. <www.hrc.co.nz/hrc_new/hrc/cms/files/documents/21-May-2009_15-42-34_Statementonlanguagepolicy.html>

Ogilvie, Sarah 2011. Linguistics, Lexicography, and the Revitalization of Endangered Languages. *International Journal of Lexicography* 24/4, 389-404.
Oommen, T. K. 2003. Language and Nation: For a Cultural Renewal of India. *Asian Journal of Social Science* 31/2: 286-303.
Paauw, Scott 2009. One Land, One Nation, One Language: An Analysis of Indonesia's National Language Policy. In Lehnert-LeHouillier, H. / Fine. A. B. (eds) *University of Rochester Working Papers in the Language Sciences* 5/1: 2-16.
Patel, Vikram 2011. Traditional Healers for Mental Health Care in Africa. *Global Health Action* 4, 1-2.
Peal, Elizabeth / Lambert, Wallace 1962. The Relation of Bilingualism to Intelligence. *Psychological Monographs* 76, 1-23.
Person, Kirk 2005. Language Revitalization or Dying Gasp? Language Preservation Efforts among the Bisu of Northern Thailand. *International Journal of the Sociology of Language* 173, 117-141.
Person, Kirk 2011. Language Policy in Thailand: Historical Background and Current Work of Royal Institute of Thailand. In *Current Status and Prospects of the Language Policies in the World.* Proceedings of the International Academic Conference for the Commemoration of the 20th Anniversary of the National Institute of the Korean Language. Seoul: National Institute of the Korean Language, 127-147.
Polinsky, Maria / Smith, Geoffrey. 2003. Pacific. In Comrie, Bernard / Matthews, Stephen / Polinsky, Maria (eds) *Atlas of Languages: The Origins and Development of Languages Throughout the World*. Sydney: ABC Books, 90-107.
Premsrirat, Suwilai 2007. Endangered Languages of Thailand. *International Journal of the Sociology of Language* 186, 75-93.
Reyes, Iliana 2009. An Ecological Perspective on Minority and Majority Language and Literacy Communities in the Americas. *Colombian Linguistic Applied Journal* 11/1, 106-114.
Robinson, Daniel 2007. *Governance and Micro-politics of Traditional Knowledge, Biodiversity and Intellectual Property in Thailand*. Bangkok: National Human Rights Commission of Thailand.

Roth, Robin 2004. Spatial Organization of Environmental Knowledge: Conservation Conflicts in the Inhabited Forest of Northern Thailand. *Ecology and Society* 9/3, 5.
Shell, Marc 1993. Babel in America; Or, the Politics of Language Diversity in the United States. *Critical Inquiry* 20, 103-127.
Spolsky, Bernard 2004. *Language Policy*. Cambridge: Cambridge University Press.
Stickel, Gerhard (ed.) 2011. *National, Regional and Minority Languages in Europe*. Contributions to the Annual Conference 2009 of EFNIL in Dublin, Frankfurt am Main.
Sumbuk, Kenneth 2006. Papua New Guinea's Languages: Will They Survive? In Cunningham, Denis / Ingram, David / Sumbuk, Kenneth (eds) *Language Diversity in the Pacific: Endangerment and Survival*. Clevedon: Multilingual Matters, 85-96.
Tchindjang, Mesmin / Bopda, Athanase / Ngamgne, Louise Angéline 2008. Languages and Cultural Identities in Africa. *Museum International* 60/3, 37-50.
Terborg, Roland / Landa, Laura García / Moore, Pauline 2006. The Language Situation in Mexico. *Current Issues in Language Planning* 7/4, 415-518.
Thomason, Sarah 2001. *Language Contact: An Introduction*. Edinburgh: Edinburgh University Press.
Timpson, Annis May (ed.) 2009. *First Nations, First Thoughts: The Impact of the Indigenous Thought in Canada*. Vancouver: UBC Press.
Troy, Jakelin / Walsh, Michael 2008. Terminology Planning in Aboriginal Australia. In Liddicoat, Anthony / Baldauf, Richard Jr (eds) *Language Planning in Local Contexts*. Clevedon, UK: Multilingual Matters, 156-170.
Tryon, Darrell 2006. Language Endangerment and Globalisation in the Pacific. In Cunningham, Denis / Ingram, David / Sumbuk, Kenneth (eds) *Language Diversity in the Pacific: Endangerment and Survival*. Clevedon: Multilingual Matters, 97-111.
Tryon, Darrell 2010. The Endangered Languages of Vanuatu. In Senft, Gunter (ed.) *Endangered Austronesian and Australian*

Aboriginal Languages: Essays on Language Documentation, Archiving and Revitalization. Canberra: Pacific Linguistics, 17-33.

United Nations Declaration on the Rights of Indigenous Peoples 2006. <www.un.org/esa/socdev/unpfii/documents/DRIPS_en.pdf>

Universal Declaration on Cultural Diversity 2001. <unesdoc.unesco.org/images/0012/001271/127160m.pdf>

Universal Declaration of Linguistic Rights 1996. <www.unesco.org/cpp/uk/declarations/linguistic.pdf>

Vakhtin, Nikolai, 1998. Endangered Languages in Northeast Siberia: Siberian Yupik and other Languages of Tchoukotka. In Kasten, Erich (ed.), *Bicultural Education in the North.* Munster: Waxmann, 159-173.

Valijärvi, Riitta-Liisa / Wilbur, Joshua 2011. The past, present and future of the Pite Saami language: Sociological factors and revitalization efforts. *Nordic Journal of Linguistics* 34/3, 295-329.

Walsh, Michael 2003. Raising Babel: Language Revitalization in New South Wales, Australia. In Blythe, Joe / McKenna Brown, Robert (eds) *Maintaining the Links: Language, Identity and the Land.* Bath: Foundation for Endangered Languages, 113-117.

Warner, Sam L. No'eau 2001. The Movement to Revitalize Hawaiian Language and Culture. In Hinton, Leanne / Hale, Ken (eds) *The Green Book of Language Revitalization in Practice.* San Diego: Academic Press, 133-146.

Whalen, Douglas / Simons, Gary 2012. Endangered Language Families. *Language* 88/1, 155-173.

Whaley, Lindsay 2011. Some Ways to Endanger an Endangered Language Project. *Language and Education* 25/4, 339-348.

Willerslev, Rane 2007. *Soul Hunters: Hunting, Animism, and Personhood among the Siberian Yukaghirs.* Berkeley: University of California Press.

Index

Agriculture, 15, 103
Ancestor, 51, 53, 63-64, 71, 77, 83, 96, 114-115, 119-120, 122-123
Animal, 11, 13, 64, 101, 104-105, 107-109, 111-113, 115, 123
Assimilation, 34, 52, 58, 61-62, 66, 68-69
Attitude, 11, 15, 22, 44, 48, 52, 54, 64, 68, 80-82, 86, 88, 91, 96-97, 99, 102, 106, 112, 122, 125-126

Belief
  animist, 62, 111, 114-115
  religious, 13, 15, 24, 37-38, 44, 52, 61, 65, 68, 71, 78, 87, 98, 113-121
  shamanistic, 64
  spiritual, 9, 11, 13-14, 71-72, 89, 100, 102, 106-107, 111, 123
  system, 9, 11, 13-15, 111-115, 118-119, 123-124
  traditional, 64, 111, 120
Birth, 93, 107, 117
Boarding school, 68
Books, 9, 11-13, 15, 22, 48, 82-83, 91, 93, 95, 102, 118-119, 126

Children, 9, 14, 20-21, 29, 32, 41, 44, 48, 51-52, 54, 60-61, 65, 68-69, 76, 79-80, 85-88, 91, 93, 95-96, 98, 107, 116-117, 121, 125-126
Civilization, 68, 73
Colonial
  authority, 62
  domain, 73-74
  era, 67, 69
  power, 13, 25, 67, 73, 88

Communication, 19, 21, 23, 26, 43, 52, 58, 64-65, 76, 79, 91-92, 99, 123
Community, 9-15, 19-20, 22, 24, 29, 34, 40, 42, 48, 51, 52-53, 56, 58, 65-67, 69, 71, 76, 79, 81-87, 89-90, 93-94, 96, 99-102, 104-105, 107-108, 110-113, 116, 118, 123-127
Conflict, 84, 111, 112, 124
Contact, 9, 17, 19, 22, 45, 52, 54, 57-58, 63, 66, 69, 77, 92-93, 96-97, 100, 106, 112, 114, 116, 120, 122, 124
Conservation, 53, 58, 99, 120
Culture, 9-13, 15, 22, 24, 28, 37, 39, 44, 52, 55, 58, 60-62, 64-68, 70-72, 77-83, 85-90, 93-101, 103, 105, 111-112, 116, 118-127
Curriculum, 88, 90, 92
Custom, 9, 13-14, 58, 62, 68, 111

Deaf, 52-53
Declaration
  international, 67, 70
  regional, 70
Development
  economic, 66
  language, 84
  rural, 119
  social, 15
Dictionary, 82-83, 91, 93-95, 102, 104-105, 108, 110, 126
Diet, 106-107
Discrimination, 52, 65, 67, 76

Ecology, 10-12, 15, 71, 101, 105, 108
Economic, 15, 44, 52, 57, 66-67, 87-88, 96, 105, 126-127

Education
  adult, 70
  bilingual, 29, 55, 76-77, 86
  dual-language, 80, 85-86
  immersion, 28, 81, 85-86, 88, 125
  mother tongue-based, 14, 20, 29, 41, 53, 65, 71, 73, 79, 85, 90-91, 93-94, 105, 119, 124-125
  multilingual, 14, 19, 27, 32, 38, 45, 57, 61, 66, 71, 73, 79, 84-87, 90, 92-94, 125-126
  pre-school, 39, 70, 89-90, 98
  primary, 39, 41, 48, 70, 88-91, 94-95, 98
  secondary, 39, 70, 88-90, 98, 115, 120
  tertiary, 70, 90
  vocational, 70, 85, 126
Elderly, 38, 51, 81, 102, 127
Elders, 9, 30, 69, 89, 96-97, 104, 111, 118
Employment, 65-66, 69
Ethnographer, 17, 22, 80, 112-113, 126
Examination, 65, 85, 105, 119

Fertility, 111-112
Food, 13, 103, 105, 107-108, 116-117, 119, 123
Forest, 11-12, 15, 103-104, 114-115, 117
Funding, 76, 79-80, 83

Grammar, 83, 90, 94-95, 124
Grandparent, 20-22, 97

Healer, 118
Health, 45, 48, 72, 77, 102, 104-105, 107, 113, 116-118
Home, 17, 20, 22-23, 27, 35, 39, 41-44, 54, 66-69, 76, 85-86, 89, 91, 93, 96-97, 99, 103, 107, 114-115, 124, 126
Human, 12-13, 19, 71, 77-78, 101-103, 110-113, 121, 123-124

Hunting, 45, 62, 64, 68, 103, 106, 109, 115, 123
Hunter-gatherer, 45, 62, 103, 109, 115, 123

Identity, 11, 15, 22, 28-29, 34-35, 38, 43-44, 57, 60, 62, 68-70, 77, 79, 83-87, 89, 91, 97, 111-112, 116, 118-122, 124, 126-127
Illness, 102, 106-107, 115, 117, 123
Independence, 29, 37, 44, 73-74
Intergenerational, 10, 20-22, 51, 59, 61, 64, 69, 82, 104, 106, 124
Internet, 111-112
Isolation, 9, 17, 19, 42, 56, 76, 88, 100, 112, 115, 127

Kinship, 111, 116
Knowledge
  ecological, 10-12, 15, 71, 101, 105, 108
  ethnobiological, 104
  environmental, 12-13, 71, 77, 87, 101, 103, 106-108, 110, 113-114, 123-124, 126-127
  herbal, 116
  medicinal, 11-12, 101, 105, 107, 110, 117
  oral, 13, 20, 94, 99, 101, 123-124
  system, 10-13, 15, 71, 101-105, 107-111, 119
  traditional, 10, 71, 93, 101-105, 107, 110, 120

Land, 12, 15, 22, 52, 54, 56, 60, 96, 101-102, 109, 112-114, 120, 123
Language
  community, 9-11, 19, 65-66, 81-82, 100, 104, 107
  creole, 32, 43, 46, 74, 87
  distinctiveness, 19, 44, 89
  diversity, 18, 24, 57, 67, 80
  documentation, 80, 104, 106, 121,

142

125
domain, 10, 51, 61, 67, 69, 73-74, 81-83, 85-87, 102, 124, 126
dominant, 44, 47, 51, 56, 66, 74, 85-86, 89, 96, 110, 112, 120, 125
endangered, 9, 11, 15, 24-26, 29-30, 32, 36-38, 40-42, 44-48, 51-52, 59, 77, 81, 99, 102, 105, 110, 112, 126
extinction, 10, 12, 17, 19, 35, 48, 58-59, 82, 90
first, 20, 32, 52, 76, 84, 86, 94
foreign, 86, 92
heritage, 9-10, 14-15, 22, 28-29, 34, 41, 56-58, 60, 64, 66-67, 76, 79-80, 85-87, 90, 93, 96, 106, 112, 122, 125-126
indigenous, 10-12, 14, 19, 26, 28-30, 32, 36, 45, 48, 51, 53-56, 58, 67-68, 70, 73, 76-78, 80, 84, 87, 90, 97, 108, 125
living, 17-18, 23-27, 29-30, 32, 35-37, 39-40, 42-45, 47
local, 27, 29, 43-44, 59-61, 63, 66, 68, 73-75, 80, 82, 85-87, 90, 92-93, 96, 94-100, 110
loss, 11, 15, 49, 54, 59, 65, 68-69, 83-84, 89-90, 96-98, 119, 125, 127
minority, 11, 28, 34-35, 38-43, 57, 63, 66-67, 70, 72-73, 79, 95-96, 110, 122, 125
national, 26, 29, 35-36, 38-40, 73-74, 76, 91
native, 72, 76, 87, 121
nest, 88
official, 24-26, 29, 40, 55, 74-75, 77, 89
pidgin, 24-25, 33, 36, 43-44, 46-47, 56-57, 59, 74, 87
policy, 11, 14, 36, 38, 67, 72-73, 77, 79, 86, 95, 122, 125-126
regional, 24-25, 27, 37, 73, 120

revitalization, 9-11, 15, 34, 38, 40, 55, 77, 80-81, 83-84, 89-90, 94, 97, 99, 108, 120, 125-126
revival, 15, 43, 49, 69, 89, 126
rights, 70, 78
scale, 20-22, 57
second, 40-41, 49, 82, 86, 94
shift, 15, 29, 43-44, 48-49, 51, 53, 56-60, 75, 83, 96-97, 124
sign, 33, 36, 52-53, 78, 89, 124-125
status, 21, 26, 40, 55, 73, 77, 89, 95
suppression, 56, 67-68
survey, 81
terminology, 102, 106, 108, 110
threat, 9, 15, 52, 59, 61-62, 64, 81, 83, 120
transmission, 11-12, 20, 22, 48, 51-52, 59, 61, 82, 101, 106, 125
use, 22, 28-29, 32, 38, 49, 51-52, 54-55, 57-58, 66-68, 82-84, 86, 92-93, 104, 108, 116, 118, 124, 126
vitality, 10, 20, 22, 44, 51, 58
Legend, 53
Lexicon, 101
Linguist, 9, 11, 17, 48, 66-67, 82, 84, 106, 122, 125
Literacy, 20, 44, 57, 62, 82, 88, 93-94, 119, 123
Longhouse, 64

Master-apprentice program, 82, 98-99
Migration, 17, 32, 41, 52, 75, 100
Missionary, 10, 44, 106, 120

Nationalism, 67, 125
Nomad, 123

Orthography, 9-10, 82-83, 93-94, 126
Ownership, 22, 54, 84

Paradigm, 14, 86, 89, 121
Parent, 21, 44, 52, 60, 64, 69, 87-88, 96-97

143

Place name, 102, 108-110, 124
Pregnancy, 116-117
Pride, 9, 11, 57, 60, 69, 77, 87, 89, 91, 99, 105, 122, 126

Reciprocity, 110, 113
Research center, 93, 122
Resistance, 57, 68, 88, 116
Repression, 30, 52
Respect, 24, 58, 71-73, 87, 91, 96, 110-116, 122, 133
Rights, 22, 52, 67, 70, 72, 77-79, 120, 125
Ritual, 53, 58, 69, 101, 103, 111-112, 116, 118, 120-121, 123-124

Schooling, 14, 22, 29-30, 34, 39-41, 43, 53, 55-57, 60-66, 68-70, 74-76, 79, 82, 84-93, 96-99, 105, 111, 120, 122, 125-126
Self-determination, 119, 127
Social
   capital, 19
   cohesion, 123
   collapse, 113
   contact, 17, 19, 57
   harmony, 113
   identity, 119
   isolation, 17
   memory, 108
   practice, 83, 111
   rules, 111
   settings, 65, 124
   standing, 62
   upheaval, 76
   values, 123, 126
Spiritual, 71-72, 102, 107, 111, 113-118, 120-121, 123
Storytelling, 13, 53, 123
Survival, 10, 13, 52, 113, 119, 125
Sustainability, 71, 101, 103-104, 110, 112-113, 123, 127

Taboo, 104, 115-116, 118, 123
Teacher, 82, 85-88, 90, 93-95, 97-98, 120-122, 126
Technology, 67, 112, 126
Trade, 61, 103, 105-106, 115

Understanding
   shared, 101

Values, 83, 101, 111, 123-124, 126

War, 69
Water, 113-115, 119, 123
Wisdom, 101

Index of languages

A'ou, 38
Abaga, 45
Abenaki-Penobscot (see also Abenaki, Eastern), 10, 51
Abenaki, Eastern, 32
Abenaki, Western, 32
Abkhaz-Adyghean, 41
Afrikaans, 78
Afro-Asiatic, 23, 25
Afro-Seminole Creole, 32
Ahom, 37
Ainu, 10, 51
Aje, 59
Akha, 55
Akposso, 107
Akum, 25
Algonquian 108
Alonquian, 28
Altai, 60
Amanayé, 30
American Sign Language, 53
Amharic, 74
Amurdak, 46
Andean-Equatorial, 28
Anindilyakwa, 46
Aore, 44, 59
Apache, Lipan, 32
Apiaká, 30
Arab Shuwa, 25
Arabic, 19, 24, 61, 74
Araki, 44, 48, 59
Arapaso, 30
Arára, Mato Grosso, 30
Arawakan, 54
Arrernte, 46
Aslian, 104
Assamese, 75

Athabascan-Eyak-Tlingit, 53
Atin, 59
Atorada, 30
Atsugewi, 32
Austro-Asiatic, 37, 55, 92
Austronesian, 47, 55, 63, 92
Awabakal, 46
Ayizi, 38

Bahasa Indonesia, 36, 75, 120
Bahasa Melayu, 74
Baissa Fali, 25
Baldemu, 26
Barbareño, 32
Baré, 30
Barikanchi, 25
Basaa, 25
Basque, 40
Bassa-Kontagora, 25
Batek, 104
Belait, 63
Beleru, 59
Bengali, 19, 75
Bengkala Sign Language, 36
Beti, 25
Bieria, 59
Bininj Gun-wok, 46
Biri, 46
Bisaya, 63
Bislama, 43-44, 47, 59, 73-74
Bisu, 56, 92-93, 100, 114-115
Blaikman Tok, 45
Boguru, 26
Bohtan Neo-Aramaic, 41
Bombara-Malinka, 24
Bot, 59
Broome Pearling Lugger Pidgin, 46

Bulu, 25
Bung, 26
Burarra, 46
Buriat, 40, 60
Burmese, 74
Busuu, 26

Cantonese, 63
Catalan, 40
Catawba, 32, 68
Celtic, 40
Chamling, 37
Chapacuran, 54
Chehalis, Lower, 32
Chehalis, Upper, 32
Chemehuevi, 98
Chiapanec, 29
Chibchan, 28
Chichewa, 74
Chicomuceltec, 29
Chinantec, Chiltepec, 29
Chinese (see also Pǔtōnghuà), 19, 38, 55, 63, 95
Chinese, Min Dong, 36
Chiquitano, 30
Chitimacha, 32
Choctaw, 76
Choinumni, 98
Chong, 56, 79, 92
Chukchansi, 98
Chung, 92
Ciluba, 26
Cocama-Cocamilla, 30
Cochimi, 29
Coeur d'Alene, 10, 51
Cook Island Mäori, 78
Coos, 32
Cruzeño, 32
Cupeño, 32

Damakawa', 25
Dari, 73
Darkinyung, 46

Daruru, 59
Daungwurrung, 46
Dhungaloo, 46
Dieri, 46
Dili, 76
Dolgan, 60
Dravidian, 37
Duala, 25
Duriankere, 36
Dusner, 36
Dusun, 63

Ekarue, 59
Emilian, 42
Enga, 44
English, 19, 24-26, 28, 32, 35, 37, 44, 46, 52-53, 56-58, 61, 64, 68-69, 73-74, 76-79, 87-94, 121
Enyau, 59
Eskimo-Aleut, 28
Eskimo, Chaplinski, 60
Esselen, 33
Evenki, 41, 60
Eyak, 10, 33, 51, 53, 99

Farafi, 59
Farnanto, 59
Finnish, 73
Foochow, 63
Fort Mojave, 98
French, 24-26, 28, 35, 44, 61-62, 73-74
Frisian, 40, 42
Frisian, Eastern, 42
Frisian, Northern, 42
Fula, 24
Fulfude, 25, 61-63

Gabi-Gabi, 46
Gagana Tokelau, 78
Gamo-Ningi, 25
Ganggalida, 46
Gara, 59
Gavião, Pará, 30

Ge-Pano-Carib, 28
Gelao, Re, 38
German, 42, 72-73
Germanic, 40, 42
Gey, 26
Gilyak, 41
Gobon, 59
Great Andamanese, Mixed, 37
Guana, 30
Guapore-Mamore, 54
Gugu Badhun, 46
Gujarati, 75
Guranalum, 58
Gureng Gureng, 47

Hainanese, 63
Hakka, 63
Halkomelem, 113
Hausa-Fulani, 24
Hausa, 24-25
Hawai'i Creole (or Hawai'i Pidgin), 43, 74, 87
Hawai'i Pidgin Sign Language, 33
Hawaiian, 87-88
Hermit, 58
Hindi, 19, 37, 74-75
Hinukh, 41
Hiri Motu, 57
Hmong-Mien, 55, 92
Hmong, 55
Hokkien, 63
Hoti, 59
Hui, 38
Hungana, 26
Hupa, 98

Iban, 63-64
Ibu, 36
Igbo, 25
Iha-based Pidgin, 36
Indo-Aryan, 37
Indo-European, 40
Indonesian (see Bahasa Indonesia)

Ineseño, 33
Inupiaq, 54
Inupiaq, Inuit, 28
Inupiaq, Inuktitut, 28
Iowa-Oto, 33
Iowa, 10, 51
Iquito, 94, 105-107
Irish, 40
Isneg, 104
Italian, 42, 73
Itelmen, 41
Itokan, 28
Ixcatec, 30

Jabutí, 30
Jahai, 104
Japanese, 19
Javindo, 36

Kaimbé, 30
Kala Kawaw Ya, 46
Kala Lagaw Ya, 45
Kalmyk, 40
Kamarian, 36
Kamasa, 45, 58
Kamba, 30
Kambiwá, 30
Kaningara, 58
Kannada, 75
Kansa, 33
Kanum, Bädi, 36
Kanuri, 25
Kapinawá, 30
Karen, 55, 103, 114
Karenggapa, 47
Kariri-Xocó, 30
Kartvelian, 41
Karuk, 98
Karuwali, 47
Kashmiri, 75
Kasong, 56, 92
Kato, 33
Katukína, 30

147

Kawacha, 45
Kaxuiâna, 31
Kayeli, 36
Kedayan, 63
Kembra, 36
Kerek, 41
Ket, 41
Khakas, 38
Khamyang, 37
Khanty, 41
Khmer, Northern, 55
Khmu, 55
Khoisan, 23
Kikongo, 24, 26
Kiliwa, 30, 99
Kinyarwanda, 73
Kiswahili, 24, 26, 73-74
Kitsai, 33
Klamath-Modoc, 33
Kongo (see Kikongo)
Koraga, Mudu, 37
Krio, 24
Kubi, 25
Kulung, 37
Kumeyaay, 99
Kuy, 55
Kwanja, 61-62
Kwerisa, 36

La'bi, 26
Labu, 45
Lae, 58
Lahu, 55
Lakondê, 31
Lalngetak, 59
Lamba, 107
Lao, 91
Latu, 59
Laua, 58
Lawa, 56, 92
Lawu, 38
Lehalrup, 59
Lemerig, 48, 59

Lengilu, 36
Lenoh, 104
Lere, 25
Leti, 26
Liki, 36
Lingala, 24, 26
Lisu, 55
Lua, 55, 92
Lumbee, 33
Lun Bawang, 63-64
Luo, 26

Macro-Ge, 54
Maidu, 98
Maidu, Northeast, 33
Malaryan, 37
Malay, 63-64, 73
Malay, Bacanese, 36
Malayalam, 75
Malkolkol, 58
Mambila, 61
Man, 38
Manchu, 38
Mandan, 10, 51
Mander, 36
Manggarai, 120
Maniq, 104
Manna-Dora, 37
Mansi, 41
Māori (see Te Reo Māori)
Marathi, 75
Margu, 47
Martha's Vineyard Sign Language, 53
Mashpi, 68
Masimasi, 36
Massep, 36
Matipuhy, 31
Mattole, 33
Mayan, 28-29
Mbwere, 59
Melayu Brunei, 63
Memie, 59
Menggu, 38

Menomini, 10, 51
Menriq, 104
Meriam Mer, 45
Miami, 33
Miao, 38
Mien, 55
Miranha, 31
Miriti, 31
Miwok, Coast, 33
Miwok, Lake, 33
Miwok, Northern Sierra, 33
Miwok, Plains, 33
Mixtec, 28
Mixtec, Sindihui, 30
Mlabri, 92
Mohegan-Pequot, 33
Mohican, 68
Moiso, 59
Moklen, 55-56, 92
Mokoro, 59
Momare, 45
Mon, 55
Mongolic, 40
Mono, 98
Mor, 36
Mpi, 56, 92
Mukah, 63
Mulao, 38
Mungaka, 25
Murrinhpatha, 46
Musau, 58
Mwe'ea, 59
Mwesen, 59

Na-Dene, 28
Naati, 59
Nakanai, 58
Nakh-Dagestanian, 41
Naman, 59
Nambikwaran, 54
Namla, 36
Nanai, 38
Nanticoke, 33

Narragansett, 33
Nasarian, 48
Nasvang-Farun, 59
Natchez, 68
Natuaki, 59
Navajo, 32, 121
Ndai, 26
Ndebele, 78
Ndjébbana, 46
Ndung, 62
Nefamese, 37
Nenets, 41, 60
Nepali, 73
Nese, 59
Netavu, 59
Nethalp, 59
Nevwol, 59
New Zealand Sign Language (or Te Reo Rotarota), 78
Newoteyene, 59
Ngandi, 47
Ngen, 59
Nggasai, 59
Nhanda, 47
Niethro, 59
Niger-Congo, 23-24
Nilo-Saharan, 23
Nimbari, 26
Ningkira, 59
Nioleien, 59
Nisenan, 33
Nisvai-Vetbong, 59
Nitita, 59
Nivat, 59
Njanga, 61-62
Njav, 59
Njerep, 25
Nokanoka, 59
Nomlaki, 33
Non-Pama-Nyungan, 45
Nooksack, 33
Nottoway, 33
Novulamleg, 59

Nukuini, 31
Nusa Laut, 36
Nyahkur, 56, 92
Nyangumarta, 46

Obispeño, 33
Oblo, 26
Odia, 59
Ohlone, Northern, 33
Ohlone, Southern, 33
Olrat, 48
Omagua, 31
Onin Based Pidgin, 36
Orang Asli, 104
Oriya, 75
Oroch, 41
Oromo/Galla, 24
Osage, 10, 51
Otomi, 28
Ouma, 58

Paiute, 99
Pali, 37
Pama-Nyungan, 45
Pankararú, 31
Pano-Tacanan, 54
Papuan, 44, 47
Paranawát, 31
Parenga, 37
Patamona, 31
Patani Malay, 55, 79, 94
Pataxó Hã-Ha-Hãe, 31
Patwin, 33
Penan Benalui, 103-104, 115
Penan, 63
Petjo, 36
Pidgin English, 24-25
Plains Indian Sign Language, 33, 52-53
Polish, 73
Pomo, Central, 98
Pomo, Eastern, 33
Pomo, Northeastern, 33
Pomo, Northern, 33, 98

Pomo, Southern, 33
Portuguese, 19, 28, 30, 72, 74, 76
Potiguára, 31
Powhatan, 33
Poyanáwa, 31
Punjabi, 75
Purisimeño, 33
Pushto, 73
Pǔtōnghuà, 38, 95

Qabiao, 38
Quechua, 96-97
Quileute, 33
Quinault, 33

Ral Aru, 59
Ral Uri, 59
Rangkas, 37
Redlahtur, 59
Rema, 45
Rhaeto-Romance, 42
Romagnol, 42
Romance, 40, 42
Romansch, 73
Rongga, 120
Ruga, 37
Russian, 19, 41, 60

Sakai, 92
Salinan, 34
Salish, Straits, 34
Sambe, 25, 56, 92
Sámi, 41, 73
Sámi, Akkala, 42
Sanskrit, 75
Sare, 58
Satawalese, 116
Saterfriesisch, 42
Selkup, 41
Semnam, 104
Sene, 58
Sereer, 24
Serrano, 34

150

Sesotho sa Leboa, 78
Sesotho, 78
Setswana, 78
Shasta, 34
Shau, 25
Sheni, 25
Sindhi, 75
Sinhala, 73
Sinie, 59
Sino-Tibetan, 37, 55, 91-92
Sirenikski Eskimo (or Sirenik), 10
Siuslaw, 34
Slavic, 42
So, 56, 92
Solomons Pijin, 43, 74
Somali, 74
Songo, 24
Sorbian, 42
Sorbian, Lower, 42
Sowa, 59
Spanish, 19, 28-29, 73-74, 96, 106
Sundani, 61
Swahili (see Kiswahili)
Swati, 78
Swedish, 73

Taa, 109
Tagalaka, 47
Tahitian, 44
Tai-Kadai, 55
Tai, 92
Tamil, 73, 75
Tandia, 36
Tanoan, 28
Tape, 59
Tapeba, 31
Tarahumara, Northern, 30
Tavalpei, 59
Tawandê, 31
Te Reo Māori, 69, 77-78, 88-89, 105, 119-120
Telugu, 75
Tench, 58

Teochew, 63
Teop, 104
Thaayorre, 46
Thai, 55, 79, 90-94
Thai, Central (or Thai Klang), 90-91
Thai, Northeastern (or Lao Isan), 90-91
Thai, Northern (or Kammuang), 90-91, 93
Thai, Southern (or Paktay), 90-91
Tibeto-Burman, 55
Tibeto-Chinese (see Sino-Tibetan)
Tingguian, 104
Tingui-Boto, 31
Tiwi, 46
To, 26
Toda, 64-65
Todhzin, 41
Tok Pisin, 43, 57-58, 74
Toksiki, 59
Tolowa, 34
Tonkawa, 34
Torá, 31
Toula, 59
Tremembé, 31
Truká, 31
Tscivenda, 78
Tungusic, 40
Tunica, 34
Tupian, 54
Tupinikin, 31
Turiwára, 31
Turumsa, 45
Tuscarora, 10, 51
Tutong, 63
Tuu, 109
Tuvin, 41, 60
Tuxá, 31
Twana, 34

Uamué, 31
Ubykh, 10, 51
Uighur, 38
Ulithian, 116

151

Ullatan, 37
Umbruul, 59
Umiida, 47
Umotína, 31
Unami, 34
Unggumi, 47
Unubahe, 45
Ura, 48, 59
Urak Lawoi, 55-56, 92
Urali, 37
Uralic, 40
Urdu, 75
Usaghade, 25
Utaha, 59
Uto-Aztecan, 28

Vagahau Niue, 78
Ventureño, 34
Vevatot, 59
Viviti, 59
Vute, 61

Wadi Wadi, 47
Waka Waka, 47
Wakoná, 31
Walpiri, 46
Wampanoag, 34
Wandala, 25
Warungu, 47
Washo, 98
Wasu, 31
Wawa, 61-63
Welsh, 40, 98
Wemba Wemba, 108
Wentuk, 59
Western Desert (or Wati), 46
Wichita, 34
Wik Mungkan, 46
Wintu, 34
Wintuan, 98
Wiyot, 34
Woleaian, 116
Wolof, 24

Woria, 36
Wukchumni, 98
Wulna, 47
Wyandot, 34

Xakriabá, 31
Xetá, 31
Xhosa, 78
Xipaya, 31
Xiriâna, 31
Xitsonga, 78
Xukurú, 31

Yabaâna, 31
Yakut, 60
Yana, 68
Yanda, 47
Yangman, 47
Yapese, 116
Yarluyandi, 47
Yatay, 47
Yawijibaya, 47
Yi, 38, 95-96
Yiddish, Western, 42
Yinwum, 47
Yirandali, 47
Yitha Yitha, 47
Yokuts, 10, 51
Yolngu-Matha, 46
Yorta Yorta, 47
Yoruba, 25
Yugh, 42
Yugul, 47
Yuki, 34
Yup'ik, 51, 54
Yup'ik Alaskan, 28
Yup'ik, Siberian, 28, 51, 54
Yuyu, 47

Zang, 38
Zaparoan, 105
Zapotec, 28
Zari, 25

Zhoa, 26
Zhuang, 38
Ziriya, 25
Zoque, Tabasco, 30
Zulu, 78

Linguistic Insights

Studies in Language and Communication

This series aims to promote specialist language studies in the fields of linguistic theory and applied linguistics, by publishing volumes that focus on specific aspects of language use in one or several languages and provide valuable insights into language and communication research. A cross-disciplinary approach is favoured and most European languages are accepted.

The series includes two types of books:

- **Monographs** – featuring in-depth studies on special aspects of language theory, language analysis or language teaching.
- **Collected papers** – assembling papers from workshops, conferences or symposia.

Each volume of the series is subjected to a double peer-reviewing process.

Vol. 1   Maurizio Gotti & Marina Dossena (eds)
Modality in Specialized Texts. Selected Papers of the 1st CERLIS Conference.
421 pages. 2001. ISBN 3-906767-10-8 · US-ISBN 0-8204-5340-4

Vol. 2   Giuseppina Cortese & Philip Riley (eds)
Domain-specific English. Textual Practices across Communities and Classrooms.
420 pages. 2002. ISBN 3-906768-98-8 · US-ISBN 0-8204-5884-8

Vol. 3   Maurizio Gotti, Dorothee Heller & Marina Dossena (eds)
Conflict and Negotiation in Specialized Texts. Selected Papers of the 2nd CERLIS Conference.
470 pages. 2002. ISBN 3-906769-12-7 · US-ISBN 0-8204-5887-2

Vol. 4   Maurizio Gotti, Marina Dossena, Richard Dury, Roberta Facchinetti & Maria Lima
Variation in Central Modals. A Repertoire of Forms and Types of Usage in Middle English and Early Modern English.
364 pages. 2002. ISBN 3-906769-84-4 · US-ISBN 0-8204-5898-8

Editorial address:

Prof. Maurizio Gotti   Università di Bergamo, Facoltà di Lingue e Letterature Straniere,
Via Salvecchio 19, 24129 Bergamo, Italy
Fax: 0039 035 2052789, E-Mail: m.gotti@unibg.it

Vol. 5   Stefania Nuccorini (ed.)
        Phrases and Phraseology. Data and Descriptions.
        187 pages. 2002. ISBN 3-906770-08-7 · US-ISBN 0-8204-5933-X

Vol. 6   Vijay Bhatia, Christopher N. Candlin & Maurizio Gotti (eds)
        Legal Discourse in Multilingual and Multicultural Contexts.
        Arbitration Texts in Europe.
        385 pages. 2003. ISBN 3-906770-85-0 · US-ISBN 0-8204-6254-3

Vol. 7   Marina Dossena & Charles Jones (eds)
        Insights into Late Modern English. 2nd edition.
        378 pages. 2003, 2007.
        ISBN 978-3-03911-257-9 · US-ISBN 978-0-8204-8927-8

Vol. 8   Maurizio Gotti
        Specialized Discourse. Linguistic Features and Changing Conventions.
        351 pages. 2003, 2005.
        ISBN 3-03910-606-6 · US-ISBN 0-8204-7000-7

Vol. 9   Alan Partington, John Morley & Louann Haarman (eds)
        Corpora and Discourse.
        420 pages. 2004. ISBN 3-03910-026-2 · US-ISBN 0-8204-6262-4

Vol. 10 Martina Möllering
        The Acquisition of German Modal Particles. A Corpus-Based Approach.
        290 pages. 2004. ISBN 3-03910-043-2 · US-ISBN 0-8204-6273-X

Vol. 11 David Hart (ed.)
        English Modality in Context. Diachronic Perspectives.
        261 pages. 2003. ISBN 3-03910-046-7 · US-ISBN 0-8204-6852-5

Vol. 12 Wendy Swanson
        Modes of Co-reference as an Indicator of Genre.
        430 pages. 2003. ISBN 3-03910-052-1 · US-ISBN 0-8204-6855-X

Vol. 13 Gina Poncini
        Discursive Strategies in Multicultural Business Meetings.
        2nd edition. 338 pages. 2004, 2007.
        ISBN 978-3-03911-296-8 · US-ISBN 978-0-8204-8937-7

Vol. 14 Christopher N. Candlin & Maurizio Gotti (eds)
        Intercultural Aspects of Specialized Communication.
        2nd edition. 369 pages. 2004, 2007.
        ISBN 978-3-03911-258-6 · US-ISBN 978-0-8204-8926-1

Vol. 15 Gabriella Del Lungo Camiciotti & Elena Tognini Bonelli (eds)
        Academic Discourse. New Insights into Evaluation.
        234 pages. 2004. ISBN 3-03910-353-9 · US-ISBN 0-8204-7016-3

Vol. 16 Marina Dossena & Roger Lass (eds)
        Methods and Data in English Historical Dialectology.
        405 pages. 2004. ISBN 3-03910-362-8 · US-ISBN 0-8204-7018-X

Vol. 17 Judy Noguchi
        The Science Review Article. An Opportune Genre in
        the Construction of Science.
        274 pages. 2006. ISBN 3-03910-426-8 · US-ISBN 0-8204-7034-1

Vol. 18 Giuseppina Cortese & Anna Duszak (eds)
Identity, Community, Discourse. English in Intercultural Settings.
495 pages. 2005. ISBN 3-03910-632-5 · US-ISBN 0-8204-7163-1

Vol. 19 Anna Trosborg & Poul Erik Flyvholm Jørgensen (eds)
Business Discourse. Texts and Contexts.
250 pages. 2005. ISBN 3-03910-606-6 · US-ISBN 0-8204-7000-7

Vol. 20 Christopher Williams
Tradition and Change in Legal English. Verbal Constructions
in Prescriptive Texts.
2nd revised edition. 216 pages. 2005, 2007. ISBN 978-3-03911-444-3.

Vol. 21 Katarzyna Dziubalska-Kolaczyk & Joanna Przedlacka (eds)
English Pronunciation Models: A Changing Scene.
2nd edition. 476 pages. 2005, 2008. ISBN 978-3-03911-682-9.

Vol. 22 Christián Abello-Contesse, Rubén Chacón-Beltrán,
M. Dolores López-Jiménez & M. Mar Torreblanca-López (eds)
Age in L2 Acquisition and Teaching.
214 pages. 2006. ISBN 3-03910-668-6 · US-ISBN 0-8204-7174-7

Vol. 23 Vijay K. Bhatia, Maurizio Gotti, Jan Engberg & Dorothee Heller (eds)
Vagueness in Normative Texts.
474 pages. 2005. ISBN 3-03910-653-8 · US-ISBN 0-8204-7169-0

Vol. 24 Paul Gillaerts & Maurizio Gotti (eds)
Genre Variation in Business Letters. 2nd printing.
407 pages. 2008. ISBN 978-3-03911-681-2.

Vol. 25 Ana María Hornero, María José Luzón & Silvia Murillo (eds)
Corpus Linguistics. Applications for the Study of English.
2nd printing. 526 pages. 2006, 2008. ISBN 978-3-03911-726-0

Vol. 26 J. Lachlan Mackenzie & María de los Ángeles Gómez-González (eds)
Studies in Functional Discourse Grammar.
259 pages. 2005. ISBN 3-03910-696-1 · US-ISBN 0-8204-7558-0

Vol. 27 Debbie G. E. Ho
Classroom Talk. Exploring the Sociocultural Structure of Formal ESL Learning.
2nd edition. 254 pages. 2006, 2007. ISBN 978-3-03911-434-4

Vol. 28 Javier Pérez-Guerra, Dolores González-Álvarez, Jorge L. Bueno-Alonso
& Esperanza Rama-Martínez (eds)
'Of Varying Language and Opposing Creed'. New Insights into Late Modern English.
455 pages. 2007. ISBN 978-3-03910-788-9

Vol. 29 Francesca Bargiela-Chiappini & Maurizio Gotti (eds)
Asian Business Discourse(s).
350 pages. 2005. ISBN 3-03910-804-2 · US-ISBN 0-8204-7574-2

Vol. 30 Nicholas Brownlees (ed.)
News Discourse in Early Modern Britain. Selected Papers of CHINED 2004.
300 pages. 2006. ISBN 3-03910-805-0 · US-ISBN 0-8204-8025-8

Vol. 31 Roberta Facchinetti & Matti Rissanen (eds)
Corpus-based Studies of Diachronic English.
300 pages. 2006. ISBN 3-03910-851-4 · US-ISBN 0-8204-8040-1

Vol. 32   Marina Dossena & Susan M. Fitzmaurice (eds)
         Business and Official Correspondence. Historical Investigations.
         209 pages. 2006. ISBN 3-03910-880-8 · US-ISBN 0-8204-8352-4

Vol. 33   Giuliana Garzone & Srikant Sarangi (eds)
         Discourse, Ideology and Specialized Communication.
         494 pages. 2007. ISBN 978-3-03910-888-6

Vol. 34   Giuliana Garzone & Cornelia Ilie (eds)
         The Use of English in Institutional and Business Settings.
         An Intercultural Perspective.
         372 pages. 2007. ISBN 978-3-03910-889-3

Vol. 35   Vijay K. Bhatia & Maurizio Gotti (eds)
         Explorations in Specialized Genres.
         316 pages. 2006. ISBN 3-03910-995-2 · US-ISBN 0-8204-8372-9

Vol. 36   Heribert Picht (ed.)
         Modern Approaches to Terminological Theories and Applications.
         432 pages. 2006. ISBN 3-03911-156-6 · US-ISBN 0-8204-8380-X

Vol. 37   Anne Wagner & Sophie Cacciaguidi-Fahy (eds)
         Legal Language and the Search for Clarity / Le langage juridique et la quête de clarté.
         Practice and Tools / Pratiques et instruments.
         487 pages. 2006. ISBN 3-03911-169-8 · US-ISBN 0-8204-8388-5

Vol. 38   Juan Carlos Palmer-Silveira, Miguel F. Ruiz-Garrido &
         Inmaculada Fortanet-Gómez (eds)
         Intercultural and International Business Communication.
         Theory, Research and Teaching.
         2nd edition. 343 pages. 2006, 2008. ISBN 978-3-03911-680-5

Vol. 39   Christiane Dalton-Puffer, Dieter Kastovsky, Nikolaus Ritt &
         Herbert Schendl (eds)
         Syntax, Style and Grammatical Norms. English from 1500–2000.
         250 pages. 2006. ISBN 3-03911-181-7 · US-ISBN 0-8204-8394-X

Vol. 40   Marina Dossena & Irma Taavitsainen (eds)
         Diachronic Perspectives on Domain-Specific English.
         280 pages. 2006. ISBN 3-03910-176-0 · US-ISBN 0-8204-8391-5

Vol. 41   John Flowerdew & Maurizio Gotti (eds)
         Studies in Specialized Discourse.
         293 pages. 2006. ISBN 3-03911-178-7

Vol. 42   Ken Hyland & Marina Bondi (eds)
         Academic Discourse Across Disciplines.
         320 pages. 2006. ISBN 3-03911-183-3 · US-ISBN 0-8204-8396-6

Vol. 43   Paul Gillaerts & Philip Shaw (eds)
         The Map and the Landscape. Norms and Practices in Genre.
         256 pages. 2006. ISBN 3-03911-182-5 · US-ISBN 0-8204-8395-4

Vol. 44   Maurizio Gotti & Davide Giannoni (eds)
         New Trends in Specialized Discourse Analysis.
         301 pages. 2006. ISBN 3-03911-184-1 · US-ISBN 0-8204-8381-8

Vol. 45   Maurizio Gotti & Françoise Salager-Meyer (eds)
         Advances in Medical Discourse Analysis. Oral and Written Contexts.
         492 pages. 2006. ISBN 3-03911-185-X · US-ISBN 0-8204-8382-6

Vol. 46 Maurizio Gotti & Susan Šarcević (eds)
        Insights into Specialized Translation.
        396 pages. 2006. ISBN 3-03911-186-8 · US-ISBN 0-8204-8383-4

Vol. 47 Khurshid Ahmad & Margaret Rogers (eds)
        Evidence-based LSP. Translation, Text and Terminology.
        584 pages. 2007. ISBN 978-3-03911-187-9

Vol. 48 Hao Sun & Dániel Z. Kádár (eds)
        It's the Dragon's Turn. Chinese Institutional Discourses.
        262 pages. 2008. ISBN 978-3-03911-175-6

Vol. 49 Cristina Suárez-Gómez
        Relativization in Early English (950-1250). the Position of Relative Clauses.
        149 pages. 2006. ISBN 3-03911-203-1 · US-ISBN 0-8204-8904-2

Vol. 50 Maria Vittoria Calvi & Luisa Chierichetti (eds)
        Nuevas tendencias en el discurso de especialidad.
        319 pages. 2006. ISBN 978-3-03911-261-6

Vol. 51 Mari Carmen Campoy & María José Luzón (eds)
        Spoken Corpora in Applied Linguistics.
        274 pages. 2008. ISBN 978-3-03911-275-3

Vol. 52 Konrad Ehlich & Dorothee Heller (Hrsg.)
        Die Wissenschaft und ihre Sprachen.
        323 pages. 2006. ISBN 978-3-03911-272-2

Vol. 53 Jingyu Zhang
        The Semantic Salience Hierarchy Model. The L2 Acquisition of Psych Predicates
        273 pages. 2007. ISBN 978-3-03911-300-2

Vol. 54 Norman Fairclough, Giuseppina Cortese & Patrizia Ardizzone (eds)
        Discourse and Contemporary Social Change.
        555 pages. 2007. ISBN 978-3-03911-276-0

Vol. 55 Jan Engberg, Marianne Grove Ditlevsen, Peter Kastberg & Martin Stegu (eds)
        New Directions in LSP Teaching.
        331 pages. 2007. ISBN 978-3-03911-433-7

Vol. 56 Dorothee Heller & Konrad Ehlich (Hrsg.)
        Studien zur Rechtskommunikation.
        322 pages. 2007. ISBN 978-3-03911-436-8

Vol. 57 Teruhiro Ishiguro & Kang-kwong Luke (eds)
        Grammar in Cross-Linguistic Perspective.
        The Syntax, Semantics, and Pragmatics of Japanese and Chinese.
        304 pages. 2012. ISBN 978-3-03911-445-0

Vol. 58 Carmen Frehner
        Email – SMS – MMS
        294 pages. 2008. ISBN 978-3-03911-451-1

Vol. 59 Isabel Balteiro
        The Directionality of Conversion in English. A Dia-Synchronic Study.
        276 pages. 2007. ISBN 978-3-03911-241-8

Vol. 60 Maria Milagros Del Saz Rubio
        English Discourse Markers of Reformulation.
        237 pages. 2007. ISBN 978-3-03911-196-1

Vol. 61 Sally Burgess & Pedro Martín-Martín (eds)
English as an Additional Language in Research Publication and Communication.
259 pages. 2008. ISBN 978-3-03911-462-7

Vol. 62 Sandrine Onillon
Pratiques et représentations de l'écrit.
458 pages. 2008. ISBN 978-3-03911-464-1

Vol. 63 Hugo Bowles & Paul Seedhouse (eds)
Conversation Analysis and Language for Specific Purposes.
2nd edition. 337 pages. 2007, 2009. ISBN 978-3-0343-0045-2

Vol. 64 Vijay K. Bhatia, Christopher N. Candlin & Paola Evangelisti Allori (eds)
Language, Culture and the Law.
The Formulation of Legal Concepts across Systems and Cultures.
342 pages. 2008. ISBN 978-3-03911-470-2

Vol. 65 Jonathan Culpeper & Dániel Z. Kádár (eds)
Historical (Im)politeness.
300 pages. 2010. ISBN 978-3-03911-496-2

Vol. 66 Linda Lombardo (ed.)
Using Corpora to Learn about Language and Discourse.
237 pages. 2009. ISBN 978-3-03911-522-8

Vol. 67 Natsumi Wakamoto
Extroversion/Introversion in Foreign Language Learning.
Interactions with Learner Strategy Use.
159 pages. 2009. ISBN 978-3-03911-596-9

Vol. 68 Eva Alcón-Soler (ed.)
Learning How to Request in an Instructed Language Learning Context.
260 pages. 2008. ISBN 978-3-03911-601-0

Vol. 69 Domenico Pezzini
The Translation of Religious Texts in the Middle Ages.
428 pages. 2008. ISBN 978-3-03911-600-3

Vol. 70 Tomoko Tode
Effects of Frequency in Classroom Second Language Learning.
Quasi-experiment and stimulated-recall analysis.
195 pages. 2008. ISBN 978-3-03911-602-7

Vol. 71 Egor Tsedryk
Fusion symétrique et alternances ditransitives.
211 pages. 2009. ISBN 978-3-03911-609-6

Vol. 72 Cynthia J. Kellett Bidoli & Elana Ochse (eds)
English in International Deaf Communication.
444 pages. 2008. ISBN 978-3-03911-610-2

Vol. 73 Joan C. Beal, Carmela Nocera & Massimo Sturiale (eds)
Perspectives on Prescriptivism.
269 pages. 2008. ISBN 978-3-03911-632-4

Vol. 74 Carol Taylor Torsello, Katherine Ackerley & Erik Castello (eds)
Corpora for University Language Teachers.
308 pages. 2008. ISBN 978-3-03911-639-3

Vol.	75	María Luisa Pérez Cañado (ed.) English Language Teaching in the European Credit Transfer System. Facing the Challenge. 251 pages. 2009. ISBN 978-3-03911-654-6
Vol.	76	Marina Dossena & Ingrid Tieken-Boon van Ostade (eds) Studies in Late Modern English Correspondence. Methodology and Data. 291 pages. 2008. ISBN 978-3-03911-658-4
Vol.	77	Ingrid Tieken-Boon van Ostade & Wim van der Wurff (eds) Current Issues in Late Modern English. 436 pages. 2009. ISBN 978-3-03911-660-7
Vol.	78	Marta Navarro Coy (ed.) Practical Approaches to Foreign Language Teaching and Learning. 297 pages. 2009. ISBN 978-3-03911-661-4
Vol.	79	Qing Ma Second Language Vocabulary Acquisition. 333 pages. 2009. ISBN 978-3-03911-666-9
Vol.	80	Martin Solly, Michelangelo Conoscenti & Sandra Campagna (eds) Verbal/Visual Narrative Texts in Higher Education. 384 pages. 2008. ISBN 978-3-03911-672-0
Vol.	81	Meiko Matsumoto From Simple Verbs to Periphrastic Expressions: The Historical Development of Composite Predicates, Phrasal Verbs, and Related Constructions in English. 235 pages. 2008. ISBN 978-3-03911-675-1
Vol.	82	Melinda Dooly Doing Diversity. Teachers' Construction of Their Classroom Reality. 180 pages. 2009. ISBN 978-3-03911-687-4
Vol.	83	Victoria Guillén-Nieto, Carmen Marimón-Llorca & Chelo Vargas-Sierra (eds) Intercultural Business Communication and Simulation and Gaming Methodology. 392 pages. 2009. ISBN 978-3-03911-688-1
Vol.	84	Maria Grazia Guido English as a Lingua Franca in Cross-cultural Immigration Domains. 285 pages. 2008. ISBN 978-3-03911-689-8
Vol.	85	Erik Castello Text Complexity and Reading Comprehension Tests. 352 pages. 2008. ISBN 978-3-03911-717-8
Vol.	86	Maria-Lluisa Gea-Valor, Isabel García-Izquierdo & Maria-José Esteve (eds) Linguistic and Translation Studies in Scientific Communication. 317 pages. 2010. ISBN 978-3-0343-0069-8
Vol.	87	Carmen Navarro, Rosa Mª Rodríguez Abella, Francesca Dalle Pezze & Renzo Miotti (eds) La comunicación especializada. 355 pages. 2008. ISBN 978-3-03911-733-8

Vol. 88 Kiriko Sato
The Development from Case-Forms to Prepositional Constructions
in Old English Prose.
231 pages. 2009. ISBN 978-3-03911-763-5

Vol. 89 Dorothee Heller (Hrsg.)
Formulierungsmuster in deutscher und italienischer Fachkommunikation.
Intra- und interlinguale Perspektiven.
315 pages. 2008. ISBN 978-3-03911-778-9

Vol. 90 Henning Bergenholtz, Sandro Nielsen & Sven Tarp (eds)
Lexicography at a Crossroads. Dictionaries and Encyclopedias Today,
Lexicographical Tools Tomorrow.
372 pages. 2009. ISBN 978-3-03911-799-4

Vol. 91 Manouchehr Moshtagh Khorasani
The Development of Controversies. From the Early Modern Period
to Online Discussion Forums.
317 pages. 2009. ISBN 978-3-3911-711-6

Vol. 92 María Luisa Carrió-Pastor (ed.)
Content and Language Integrated Learning. Cultural Diversity.
178 pages. 2009. ISBN 978-3-3911-818-2

Vol. 93 Roger Berry
Terminology in English Language Teaching. Nature and Use.
262 pages. 2010. ISBN 978-3-0343-0013-1

Vol. 94 Roberto Cagliero & Jennifer Jenkins (eds)
Discourses, Communities, and Global Englishes
240 pages. 2010. ISBN 978-3-0343-0012-4

Vol. 95 Facchinetti Roberta, Crystal David, Seidlhofer Barbara (eds)
From International to Local English – And Back Again.
268 pages. 2010. ISBN 978-3-0343-0011-7

Vol. 96 Cesare Gagliardi & Alan Maley (eds)
EIL, ELF, Global English. Teaching and Learning Issues
376 pages. 2010. ISBN 978-3-0343-0010-0

Vol. 97 Sylvie Hancil (ed.)
The Role of Prosody in Affective Speech.
403 pages. 2009. ISBN 978-3-03911-696-6

Vol. 98 Marina Dossena & Roger Lass (eds)
Studies in English and European Historical Dialectology.
257 pages. 2009. ISBN 978-3-0343-0024-7

Vol. 99 Christine Béal
Les interactions quotidiennes en français et en anglais.
De l'approche comparative à l'analyse des situations interculturelles.
424 pages. 2010. ISBN 978-3-0343-0027-8

Vol. 100 Maurizio Gotti (ed.)
Commonality and Individuality in Academic Discourse.
398 pages. 2009. ISBN 978-3-0343-0023-0

Vol. 101 Javier E. Díaz Vera & Rosario Caballero (eds)
Textual Healing. Studies in Medieval English Medical, Scientific and Technical Texts.
213 pages. 2009. ISBN 978-3-03911-822-9

Vol. 102   Nuria Edo Marzá
The Specialised Lexicographical Approach. A Step further in Dictionary-making.
316 pages. 2009. ISBN 978-3-0343-0043-8

Vol. 103   Carlos Prado-Alonso, Lidia Gómez-García, Iria Pastor-Gómez &
David Tizón-Couto (eds)
New Trends and Methodologies in Applied English Language Research.
Diachronic, Diatopic and Contrastive Studies.
348 pages. 2009. ISBN 978-3-0343-0046-9

Vol. 104   Françoise Salager-Meyer & Beverly A. Lewin
Crossed Words. Criticism in Scholarly Writing?
371 pages. 2011. ISBN 978-3-0343-0049-0.

Vol. 105   Javier Ruano-García
Early Modern Northern English Lexis. A Literary Corpus-Based Study.
611 pages. 2010. ISBN 978-3-0343-0058-2

Vol. 106   Rafael Monroy-Casas
Systems for the Phonetic Transcription of English. Theory and Texts.
280 pages. 2011. ISBN 978-3-0343-0059-9

Vol. 107   Nicola T. Owtram
The Pragmatics of Academic Writing.
A Relevance Approach to the Analysis of Research Article Introductions.
311 pages. 2009. ISBN 978-3-0343-0060-5

Vol. 108   Yolanda Ruiz de Zarobe, Juan Manuel Sierra &
Francisco Gallardo del Puerto (eds)
Content and Foreign Language Integrated Learning.
Contributions to Multilingualism in European Contexts
343 pages. 2011. ISBN 978-3-0343-0074-2

Vol. 109   Ángeles Linde López & Rosalía Crespo Jiménez (eds)
Professional English in the European context. The EHEA challenge.
374 pages. 2010. ISBN 978-3-0343-0088-9

Vol. 110   Rosalía Rodríguez-Vázquez
The Rhythm of Speech, Verse and Vocal Music. A New Theory.
394 pages. 2010. ISBN 978-3-0343-0309-5

Vol. 111   Anastasios Tsangalidis & Roberta Facchinetti (eds)
Studies on English Modality. In Honour of Frank Palmer.
392 pages. 2009. ISBN 978-3-0343-0310-1

Vol. 112   Jing Huang
Autonomy, Agency and Identity in Foreign Language Learning and Teaching.
400 pages. 2013. ISBN 978-3-0343-0370-5

Vol. 113   Mihhail Lotman & Maria-Kristiina Lotman (eds)
Frontiers in Comparative Prosody. In memoriam: Mikhail Gasparov.
426 pages. 2011. ISBN 978-3-0343-0373-6

Vol. 114   Merja Kytö, John Scahill & Harumi Tanabe (eds)
Language Change and Variation from Old English to Late Modern English.
A Festschrift for Minoji Akimoto
422 pages. 2010. ISBN 978-3-0343-0372-9

Vol. 115   Giuliana Garzone & Paola Catenaccio (eds)
Identities across Media and Modes. Discursive Perspectives.
379 pages. 2009. ISBN 978-3-0343-0386-6

Vol. 116 Elena Landone
Los marcadores del discurso y cortesía verbal en español.
390 pages. 2010. ISBN 978-3-0343-0413-9

Vol. 117 Maurizio Gotti & Christopher Williams (eds)
Legal Discourse across Languages and Cultures.
339 pages. 2010. ISBN 978-3-0343-0425-2

Vol. 118 David Hirsh
Academic Vocabulary in Context.
217 pages. 2010. ISBN 978-3-0343-0426-9

Vol. 119 Yvonne Dröschel
Lingua Franca English. The Role of Simplification and Transfer.
358 pages. 2011. ISBN 978-3-0343-0432-0

Vol. 120 Tengku Sepora Tengku Mahadi, Helia Vaezian & Mahmoud Akbari
Corpora in Translation. A Practical Guide.
135 pages. 2010. ISBN 978-3-0343-0434-4

Vol. 121 Davide Simone Giannoni & Celina Frade (eds)
Researching Language and the Law. Textual Features and Translation Issues.
278 pages. 2010. ISBN 978-3-0343-0443-6

Vol. 122 Daniel Madrid & Stephen Hughes (eds)
Studies in Bilingual Education.
472 pages. 2011. ISBN 978-3-0343-0474-0

Vol. 123 Vijay K. Bhatia, Christopher N. Candlin & Maurizio Gotti (eds)
The Discourses of Dispute Resolution.
290 pages. 2010. ISBN 978-3-0343-0476-4

Vol. 124 Davide Simone Giannoni
Mapping Academic Values in the Disciplines. A Corpus-Based Approach.
288 pages. 2010. ISBN 978-3-0343-0488-7

Vol. 125 Giuliana Garzone & James Archibald (eds)
Discourse, Identities and Roles in Specialized Communication.
419 pages. 2010. ISBN 978-3-0343-0494-8

Vol. 126 Iria Pastor-Gómez
The Status and Development of N+N Sequences in
Contemporary English Noun Phrases.
216 pages. 2011. ISBN 978-3-0343-0534-1

Vol. 127 Carlos Prado-Alonso
Full-verb Inversion in Written and Spoken English.
261 pages. 2011. ISBN 978-3-0343-0535-8

Vol. 128 Tony Harris & María Moreno Jaén (eds)
Corpus Linguistics in Language Teaching.
214 pages. 2010. ISBN 978-3-0343-0524-2

Vol. 129 Tetsuji Oda & Hiroyuki Eto (eds)
Multiple Perspectives on English Philology and History of Linguistics.
A Festschrift for Shoichi Watanabe on his 80th Birthday.
378 pages. 2010. ISBN 978-3-0343-0480-1

Vol. 130   Luisa Chierichetti & Giovanni Garofalo (eds)
Lengua y Derecho. líneas de investigación interdisciplinaria.
283 pages. 2010. 978-3-0343-0463-4

Vol. 131   Paola Evangelisti Allori & Giuliana Garzone (eds)
Discourse, Identities and Genres in Corporate Communication.
Sponsorship, Advertising and Organizational Communication.
324 pages. 2011. 978-3-0343-0591-4

Vol. 132   Leyre Ruiz de Zarobe & Yolanda Ruiz de Zarobe (eds)
Speech Acts and Politeness across Languages and Cultures.
402 pages. 2012. 978-3-0343-0611-9

Vol. 133   Thomas Christiansen
Cohesion. A Discourse Perspective.
387 pages. 2011. 978-3-0343-0619-5

Vol. 134   Giuliana Garzone & Maurizio Gotti
Discourse, Communication and the Enterprise. Genres and Trends.
451 pages. 2011. ISBN 978-3-0343-0620-1

Vol. 135   Zsuzsa Hoffmann
Ways of the World's Words.
Language Contact in the Age of Globalization.
334 pages 2011. ISBN 978-3-0343-0673-7

Vol. 136   Cecilia Varcasia (ed.)
Becoming Multilingual.
Language Learning and Language Policy between Attitudes and Identities.
213 pages. 2011. ISBN 978-3-0343-0687-5

Vol. 137   Susy Macqueen
The Emergence of Patterns in Second Language Writing.
A Sociocognitive Exploration of Lexical Trails.
325 pages. 2012. ISBN 978-3-0343-1010-9

Vol. 138   Maria Vittoria Calvi & Giovanna Mapelli (eds)
La lengua del turismo. Géneros discursivos y terminología.
365 pages. 2011. ISBN 978-3-0343-1011-6

Vol. 139   Ken Lau
Learning to Become a Professional in a Textually-Mediated World.
A Text-Oriented Study of Placement Practices.
261 pages. 2012. ISBN 978-3-0343-1016-1

Vol. 140   Sandra Campagna, Giuliana Garzone, Cornelia Ilie & Elizabeth Rowley-Jolivet (eds)
Evolving Genres in Web-mediated Communication.
337 pages. 2012. ISBN 978-3-0343-1013-0

Vol. 141   Edith Esch & Martin Solly (eds)
The Sociolinguistics of Language Education in International Contexts.
263 pages. 2012. ISBN 978-3-0343-1009-3

Vol. 142   Forthcoming.

Vol. 143   David Tizón-Couto
Left Dislocation in English. A Functional-Discoursal Approach.
416 pages. 2012. ISBN 978-3-0343-1037-6

Vol. 144   Margrethe Petersen & Jan Engberg (eds)
Current Trends in LSP Research. Aims and Methods.
323 pages. 2011. ISBN 978-3-0343-1054-3

Vol. 145   David Tizón-Couto, Beatriz Tizón-Couto, Iria Pastor-Gómez & Paula Rodríguez-Puente (eds)
New Trends and Methodologies in Applied English Language Research II.
Studies in Language Variation, Meaning and Learning.
283 pages. 2012. ISBN 978-3-0343-1061-1

Vol. 146   Rita Salvi & Hiromasa Tanaka (eds)
Intercultural Interactions in Business and Management.
306 pages. 2011. ISBN 978-3-0343-1039-0

Vol. 147   Francesco Straniero Sergio & Caterina Falbo (eds)
Breaking Ground in Corpus-based Interpreting Studies.
254 pages. 2012. ISBN 978-3-0343-1071-0

Vol. 148   Forthcoming.

Vol. 149   Vijay K. Bhatia & Paola Evangelisti Allori (eds)
Discourse and Identity in the Professions. Legal, Corporate and Institutional Citizenship.
352 pages. 2011. ISBN 978-3-0343-1079-6

Vol. 150   Maurizio Gotti (ed.)
Academic Identity Traits. A Corpus-Based Investigation.
363 pages. 2012. ISBN 978-3-0343-1141-0

Vol. 151   Priscilla Heynderickx, Sylvain Dieltjens, Geert Jacobs, Paul Gillaerts &
Elizabeth de Groot (eds)
The Language Factor in International Business.
New Perspectives on Research, Teaching and Practice.
320 pages. 2012. ISBN 978-3-0343-1090-1

Vol. 152   Paul Gillaerts, Elizabeth de Groot, Sylvain Dieltjens, Priscilla Heynderickx &
Geert Jacobs (eds)
Researching Discourse in Business Genres. Cases and Corpora.
215 pages. 2012. ISBN 978-3-0343-1092-5

Vol. 153   Yongyan Zheng
Dynamic Vocabulary Development in a Foreign Language.
262 pages. 2012. ISBN 978-3-0343-1106-9

Vol. 154   Carmen Argondizzo (ed.)
Creativity and Innovation in Language Education.
357 pages. 2012. ISBN 978-3-0343-1080-2

Vol. 155   David Hirsh (ed.)
Current Perspectives in Second Language Vocabulary Research.
180 pages. 2012. ISBN 978-3-0343-1108-3

Vol. 156   Seiji Shinkawa
Unhistorical Gender Assignment in Laȝamon's *Brut*. A Case Study of a Late Stage
in the Development of Grammatical Gender toward its Ultimate Loss.
186 pages. 2012. ISBN 978-3-0343-1124-3

Vol. 157   Yeonkwon Jung
Basics of Organizational Writing: A Critical Reading Approach.
151 pages. 2014. ISBN 978-3-0343-1137-3.

Vol. 158　Bárbara Eizaga Rebollar (ed.)
Studies in Linguistics and Cognition.
301 pages. 2012. ISBN 978-3-0343-1138-0

Vol. 159　Giuliana Garzone, Paola Catenaccio, Chiara Degano (eds)
Genre Change in the Contemporary World. Short-term Diachronic Perspectives.
329 pages. 2012. ISBN 978-3-0343-1214-1

Vol. 160　Carol Berkenkotter, Vijay K. Bhatia & Maurizio Gotti (eds)
Insights into Academic Genres.
468 pages. 2012. ISBN 978-3-0343-1211-0

Vol. 161　Beatriz Tizón-Couto
Clausal Complements in Native and Learner Spoken English. A corpus-based study with Lindsei and Vicolse. 357 pages. 2013. ISBN 978-3-0343-1184-7

Vol. 162　Patrizia Anesa
Jury Trials and the Popularization of Legal Language. A Discourse Analytical Approach.
247 pages. 2012. ISBN 978-3-0343-1231-8

Vol. 163　David Hirsh
Endangered Languages, Knowledge Systems and Belief Systems.
153 pages. 2013. ISBN 978-3-0343-1232-5

Vol. 164-165　Forthcoming.

Vol. 166　Rita Salvi & Janet Bowker (eds)
Space, Time and the Construction of Identity.
Discursive Indexicality in Cultural, Institutional and Professional Fields.
324 pages. 2013. ISBN 978-3-0343-1254-7

Vol. 167　Shunji Yamazaki & Robert Sigley (eds)
Approaching Language Variation through Corpora. A Festschrift in Honour of Toshio Saito.
421 pages. 2013. ISBN 978-3-0343 1264-6

Vol. 168　Franca Poppi
Global Interactions in English as a Lingua Franca. How written communication is changing under the influence of electronic media and new contexts of use.
249 pages. 2012. ISBN 978-3-0343-1276-9

Vol. 169　Miguel A. Aijón Oliva & María José Serrano
Style in syntax. Investigating variation in Spanish pronoun subjects.
239 pages. 2013. ISBN 978-3-0343-1244-8

Vol. 170　Forthcoming.

Vol. 171　Aleksandra Matulewska
Legilinguistic Translatology. A Parametric Approach to Legal Translation.
279 pages. 2013. ISBN 978-3-0343-1287-5

Vol. 172　Maurizio Gotti & Carmen Sancho Guinda (eds)
Narratives in Academic and Professional Genres.
513 pages. 2013. ISBN 978-3-0343-1371-1

Vol. 173　Forthcoming.

Vol. 174　Chihiro Inoue
Task Equivalence in Speaking Tests.
251 pages. 2013. ISBN 978-3-0343-1417-6

Vol. 175　Forthcoming.

Vol. 176 Catherine Resche
Economic Terms and Beyond: Capitalising on the Wealth of Notions.
How Researchers in Specialised Varieties of English Can Benefit from Focusing on Terms.
332 pages. 2013. ISBN 978-3-0343-1435-0

Vol. 177 Forthcoming.

Vol. 178 Cécile Desoutter & Caroline Mellet (dir.)
Le discours rapporté: approches linguistiques et perspectives didactiques.
270 pages. 2013. ISBN 978-3-0343-1292-9

Vol. 179-186 Forthcoming.

Vol. 187 Marina Bondi & Rosa Lorés Sanz (eds)
Abstracts in Academic Discourse. Variation and Change.
270 pages. 2013. ISBN 978-3-0343-1483-1